JAN. 08

Test Results for Digital Data Acquisition Tool: EnCase Linen 5.05f

NCJ 221167

David W. Hagy

Acting Principal Deputy Director, National Institute of Justice

This report was prepared for the National Institute of Justice, U.S. Department of Justice, by the Office of Law Enforcement Standards of the National Institute of Standards and Technology under Interagency Agreement 2003–IJ–R–029.

The National Institute of Justice is a component of the Office of Justice Programs, which also includes the Bureau of Justice Assistance, the Bureau of Justice Statistics, the Office of Juvenile Justice and Delinquency Prevention, and the Office for Victims of Crime.

August 7, 2007

Test Results for Digital Data Acquisition Tool:
EnCase Linen 5.05f

January 2008

National Institute of Standards and Technology
Technology Administration, U.S. Department of Commerce

Contents

Introduction

The Computer Forensics Tool Testing (CFTT) program is a joint project of the National Institute of Justice (NIJ), the research and development organization of the U.S. Department of Justice, and the National Institute of Standards and Technology's (NIST's) Office of Law Enforcement Standards and Information Technology Laboratory. CFTT is supported by other organizations, including the Federal Bureau of Investigation, the U.S. Department of Defense Cyber Crime Center, U.S. Internal Revenue Service Criminal Investigation Division Electronic Crimes Program, and the U.S. Department of Homeland Security's Bureau of Immigration and Customs Enforcement and U.S. Secret Service. The objective of the CFTT program is to provide measurable assurance to practitioners, researchers, and other applicable users that the tools used in computer forensics investigations provide accurate results. Accomplishing this requires the development of specifications and test methods for computer forensics tools and subsequent testing of specific tools against those specifications.

Test results provide the information necessary for developers to improve tools, users to make informed choices, and the legal community and others to understand the tools' capabilities. This approach to testing computer forensic tools is based on well-recognized methodologies for conformance and quality testing. The specifications and test methods are posted on the CFTT Web site (http://www.cftt.nist.gov/) for review and comment by the computer forensics community.

This document reports the results from testing EnCase Linen, version 5.05f, against the *Digital Data Acquisition Tool Assertions and Test Plan Version 1.0*, available at the CFTT Web site (http://www.cftt.nist.gov/DA-ATP-pc-01.pdf).

Test results from other software packages and the CFTT tool methodology can be found on NIJ's computer forensics tool testing Web page, http://www.ojp.usdoj.gov/nij/topics/ecrime/cftt.htm.

Test Results for Digital Data Acquisition Tool

Tool Tested: EnCase Linen
Version: 5.05f
Run Environments: Helix 1.7 Linux Boot CD, Fedora Core 5 & SuSe 10.0

Supplier: Guidance Software, Inc.

Address: 215 North Marengo Ave., Suite 250
                       Pasadena, CA 91101
Tel: 626–229–9191
Fax: 626–229–9199
WWW: http://www.guidancesoftware.com/

1   Results Summary

Except for two test cases (DA–08 and DA–09), the tested tool acquired all visible and hidden sectors completely and accurately from the test media. The two exceptions are the following:

1. Up to seven sectors contiguous to a defective sector may be replaced by zeros in the acquisition (DA–09–1 and DA–09–2).
2. The sectors hidden by a *device configuration overlay* (DCO) are not acquired (DA–08–DCO).

2   Test Case Selection

Not all test cases or test assertions are appropriate for all tools. In addition to the base test cases, each remaining test case is linked to optional tool features needed for the test case. If a given tool implements a given feature then the test cases linked to that feature are run. Table 1 lists the features available in EnCase Linen and the linked test cases. Table 2 lists the features not available in EnCase Linen and the linked test cases.

Table 1 Selected Test Cases

Supported Optional Feature	Cases selected for execution
Base Cases	06, 07 & 08
Destination Device Switching	13
Read error during acquisition	09
Create an image file in more than one format	10

Table 2 Omitted Test Cases

Unsupported Optional Feature	Cases omitted (not executed)
Create a clone during acquisition	01, 02 & 04

Create cylinder aligned clones	03, 15, 21 & 23
Convert an image file from one format to another	26
Insufficient space for image file	12
Device I/O error generator available	05, 11 & 18
Fill excess sectors on a clone device	19, 20, 21, 22 & 23
Create a clone from an image file	14 & 17
Create a clone from a subset of an image file	16
Detect a corrupted (or changed) image file	24 & 25

Some test cases have variant forms to accommodate parameters within test assertions. These variations cover the execution environment, acquisition interface to the source drive, and type of digital object acquired. Variations were also created for image file format and error granularity (test case DA–9).

The tool was executed in one of the following Linux run time environments: Helix 1.7, Fedora Core 5 or SuSe 10.0.

The following source interfaces were tested: ATA28, ATA48, SATA28, SATA48, SCSI, USB, and FireWire.

The following digital sources were tested: partitions (FAT12, FAT16, FAT32, FAT32X, EXT2, and NTFS), and thumb drive.

The image files were created on FAT32 partitions.

3 Results by Test Assertion

Table 3 summarizes the test results by assertion. The column labeled **Assertion** gives the text of each assertion. The column labeled **Tests** gives the number of test cases that use the given assertion. The column labeled **Anomaly** gives the section number in this report where the anomaly is discussed. Two test assertions only apply in special circumstances. The assertion AO–22 is checked only for tools that create block hashes. This assertion does not apply to EnCase Linen. The assertion AO–24 is only checked if the tool is executed in a run time environment that does not modify attached storage devices, such as MS DOS. In normal operation an imaging tool is used in conjunction with a write block device to protect the source drive; however a blocker was not used during the tests so that assertion AO–24 could be checked.

Table 3 Assertions Tested

Assertions Tested	Tests	Anomaly
AM–01 The tool uses access interface SRC–AI to access the digital source.	24	

AM–02 The tool acquires digital source DS.	24	
AM–03 The tool executes in execution environment XE.	24	
AM–05 If image file creation is specified, the tool creates an image file on file system type FS.	24	
AM–06 All visible sectors are acquired from the digital source.	24	
AM–07 All hidden sectors are acquired from the digital source.	3	3.1
AM–08 All sectors acquired from the digital source are acquired accurately.	24	3.2
AM–09 If unresolved errors occur while reading from the selected digital source, the tool notifies the user of the error type and location within the digital source.	4	
AM–10 If unresolved errors occur while reading from the selected digital source, the tool uses a benign fill in the destination object in place of the inaccessible data.	4	
AO–01 If the tool creates an image file, the data represented by the image file is the same as the data acquired by the tool.	24	
AO–02 If an image file format is specified, the tool creates an image file in the specified format.	1	
AO–04 If the tool is creating an image file and there is insufficient space on the image destination device to contain the image file, the tool shall notify the user.	1	
AO–05 If the tool creates a multi-file image of a requested size then all the individual files shall be no larger than the requested size.	24	
AO–10 If there is insufficient space to contain all files of a multi-file image and if destination device switching is supported, the image is continued on another device.	1	
AO–23 If the tool logs any log significant information, the information is accurately recorded in the log file.	24	
AO–24 If the tool executes in a forensically safe execution environment, the digital source is unchanged by the acquisition process.	24	

Table 4 lists the assertions that were not tested, usually due to the tool not supporting some optional feature, e.g., creation of cylinder aligned clones.

Table 4 Assertions not Tested

Assertions not Tested
AM–04 If clone creation is specified, the tool creates a clone of the digital source.
AO–03 If there is an error while writing the image file, the tool notifies the user.
AO–06 If the tool performs an image file integrity check on an image file that has not been changed since the file was created, the tool shall notify the user that the image file has not been changed.
AO–07 If the tool performs an image file integrity check on an image file that has been changed since the file was created, the tool shall notify the user that the image file has been changed.

AO–08 If the tool performs an image file integrity check on an image file that has been changed since the file was created, the tool shall notify the user of the affected locations.
AO–09 If the tool converts a source image file from one format to a target image file in another format, the acquired data represented in the target image file is the same as the acquired data in the source image file.
AO–11 If requested, a clone is created during an acquisition of a digital source.
AO–12 If requested, a clone is created from an image file.
AO–13 A clone is created using access interface DST–AI to write to the clone device.
AO–14 If an unaligned clone is created, each sector written to the clone is accurately written to the same disk address on the clone that the sector occupied on the digital source.
AO–15 If an aligned clone is created, each sector within a contiguous span of sectors from the source is accurately written to the same disk address on the clone device relative to the start of the span as the sector occupied on the original digital source. A span of sectors is defined to be either a mountable partition or a contiguous sequence of sectors not part of a mountable partition. Extended partitions, which may contain both mountable partitions and unallocated sectors, are not mountable partitions.
AO–16 If a subset of an image or acquisition is specified, all the subset is cloned.
AO–17 If requested, any excess sectors on a clone destination device are not modified.
AO–18 If requested, a benign fill is written to excess sectors of a clone.
AO–19 If there is insufficient space to create a complete clone, a truncated clone is created using all available sectors of the clone device.
AO–20 If a truncated clone is created, the tool notifies the user.
AO–21 If there is a write error during clone creation, the tool notifies the user.
AO–22 If requested, the tool calculates block hashes for a specified block size during an acquisition for each block acquired from the digital source.

3.1 Acquisition of HPA and DCO

The tool does not remove either Host Protected Areas (HPAs) or DCOs. However, the Linux test environment automatically removed the HPA on the test drive, allowing the tool to image sectors hidden by an HPA. The tool did not acquire sectors hidden by a DCO.

3.2 Acquisition of Faulty Sectors

For each variation of test case DA–09 some readable sectors as acquired to the image file differed from the source drive. To determine which sectors were accurately acquired, the image file was restored to a clone using EnCase 5.05f and the clone was compared to the source drive.

Linen 5.05f allows the user to specify a granularity value for an acquisition. The value specifies the number of sectors that the tool should zero fill surrounding and including a faulty sector if a read error is encountered during acquisition. If a granularity greater than 1 is specified, some readable sectors may be replaced with zeros in the image file. This is a design decision in the tool that trades off zeroing the content of sectors near a faulty sector for a faster acquisition.

For test cases DA–09–01 and DA–09–02 (granularity values of 1 and 2), the actual number of zeroed sectors was 8 rather than the specified granularity value.

For tested granularity values greater than 8 the number of zeroed sectors was as documented for the specified granularity with some readable sectors in the image file filled with zeros.

It should be noted that only the ATA interface on Linux (kernel version 2.6) was used in the testing. Other interfaces, e.g., USB, Firewire or SCSI, or other versions of Linux, may exhibit other behavior in variations DA–09–01 and DA–09–02.

4 Testing Environment

The tests were run in the NIST CFTT lab. This section describes the test computers available for testing.

4.1 Test Computers

Five test computers were used.

Joe and **Max** have the following configuration:

Intel® Desktop Motherboard D865GB/D865PERC (with ATA–6 IDE on board controller)
BIOS Version BF86510A.86A.0053.P13
Adaptec SCSI BIOS V3.10.0
Intel® Pentium™ 4 CPU 3.4Ghz
2577972KB RAM
SONY DVD RW DRU–530A, ATAPI CD/DVD–ROM drive
1.44 MB floppy drive
Two slots for removable IDE hard disk drives
Two slots for removable SATA hard disk drives
Two slots for removable SCSI hard disk drives

Paladin and **AndWife** have the following configuration:

Intel® D845WNL Motherboard
BIOS Version HV84510A.86A.0022.P05
Intel® Pentium™ 4 CPU 2.0Ghz
512672K RAM
Adaptec 29160 SCSI Adapter card
Tekram DC–390U3W SCSI Adapter card
Plextor CR–RW PX–W124TS Rev: 1.06

LG 52X CDROM
1.44 MB floppy drive
Three slots for removable IDE hard disk drives
Two slots for removable SCSI hard disk drive

Aramis has the following configuration:

Shuttle SD37P2 Motherboard
BIOS Phoenix Award
Intel® Core™2 Duo Core 2 775 CPU 1.86GHz
Memory (4) 240 pin DDR2 DIMM slots
3x2GB (2 GB 240–pin PC2–4200 non-ECC DDR2 non-Registered DIMM (p/n AMF)
per DIMM (Max 6 GB)
1x512 MB (1 512MB 240–pin)
Lite-on IT Corp Model CD–RW/DVD–ROM SOHC–5236V Drive
3–port FireWire 800 (2x 9–pin, 1x 6–pin) PCI Express x1 card. RoHS compliant.
8 USB 2.0 ports
1 IEEE 1394 port (Mini)
1 IEEE 1394 port
1 External SATA port
1 RJ45 Gigabit LAN port
1 Coaxial S/PDIF out

4.2 Support Software

A package of programs to support test analysis, FS–TST Release 2.0, was used. The
software can be obtained from: http://www.cftt.nist.gov/diskimaging/fs-tst20.zip.

5   Test Results

The main item of interest for interpreting the test results is determining the conformance
of the device with the test assertions. Conformance with each assertion tested by a given
test case is evaluated by examining **Log File Highlights** box of the test report summary.

5.1 Test Results Report Key

A summary of the actual test results is presented in this report. The following table
presents a description of each section of the test report summary.

Heading	Description
First Line:	Test case ID, name, and version of tool tested.
Case Summary:	Test case summary from *Digital Data Acquisition Tool Assertions and Test Plan Version 1.0*.
Assertions:	The test assertions applicable to the test case, selected from *Digital Data Acquisition Tool Assertions and Test Plan Version 1.0*.

Heading	Description
Tester Name:	Name or initials of person executing test procedure.
Test Host:	Host computer executing the test.
Test Date:	Time and date that test was started.
Drives:	Source drive (the drive acquired), destination drive (if a clone is created) and media drive (to contain a created image).
Source Setup:	Layout of partitions on the source drive and the expected hash of the drive.
Log Highlights:	Information extracted from various log files to illustrate conformance or nonconformance to the test assertions.
Results	Expected and actual results for each assertion tested.
Analysis	Whether or not the expected results were achieved.

5.2 Test Details

5.2.1 DA-06-ATA28

Test Case DA-06-ATA28 Linen 5.05f	
Case Summary:	DA-06 Acquire a physical device using access interface AI to an image file.
Assertions:	AM-01 The tool uses access interface SRC-AI to access the digital source. AM-02 The tool acquires digital source DS. AM-03 The tool executes in execution environment XE. AM-05 If image file creation is specified, the tool creates an image file on file system type FS. AM-06 All visible sectors are acquired from the digital source. AM-08 All sectors acquired from the digital source are acquired accurately. AO-01 If the tool creates an image file, the data represented by the image file is the same as the data acquired by the tool. AO-05 If the tool creates a multi-file image of a requested size then all the individual files shall be no larger than the requested size. AO-22 If requested, the tool calculates block hashes for a specified block size during an acquisition for each block acquired from the digital source. AO-23 If the tool logs any log significant information, the information is accurately recorded in the log file. AO-24 If the tool executes in a forensically safe execution environment, the digital source is unchanged by the acquisition process.
Tester Name:	brl
Test Host:	Max
Test Date:	Thu Jan 4 11:58:47 2007
Drives:	src(43) dst (none) other (EF)
Source Setup:	src hash (SHA1): < 888E2E7F7AD237DC7A732281DD93F325065E5871 > src hash (MD5): < BC39C3F7EE7A50E77B9BA1E65A5AEEF7 > 78125000 total sectors (40000000000 bytes) Model (0BB-75JHC0) serial # (WD-WMAMC46588) <pre> N Start LBA Length Start C/H/S End C/H/S boot Partition type
1 P 000000063 020980827 0000/001/01 1023/254/63   0C Fat32X
2 X 020980890 057143205 1023/000/01 1023/254/63   0F extended
3 S 000000063 000032067 1023/001/01 1023/254/63   01 Fat12
4 x 000032130 002104515 1023/000/01 1023/254/63   05 extended
5 S 000000063 002104452 1023/001/01 1023/254/63   06 Fat16
6 x 002136645 004192965 1023/000/01 1023/254/63   05 extended
7 S 000000063 004192902 1023/001/01 1023/254/63   16 other
8 x 006329610 008401995 1023/000/01 1023/254/63   05 extended
9 S 000000063 008401932 1023/001/01 1023/254/63   0B Fat32
10 x 014731605 010490445 1023/000/01 1023/254/63   05 extended
11 S 000000063 010490382 1023/001/01 1023/254/63   83 Linux
12 x 025222050 004209030 1023/000/01 1023/254/63   05 extended
13 S 000000063 004208967 1023/001/01 1023/254/63   82 Linux swap
14 x 029431080 027712125 1023/000/01 1023/254/63   05 extended
15 S 000000063 027712062 1023/001/01 1023/254/63   07 NTFS
16 S 000000000 000000000 0000/000/00 0000/000/00   00 empty entry
17 P 000000000 000000000 0000/000/00 0000/000/00   00 empty entry
18 P 000000000 000000000 0000/000/00 0000/000/00   00 empty entry
1 020980827 sectors 10742183424 bytes
3 000032067 sectors 16418304 bytes
5 002104452 sectors 1077479424 bytes
7 004192902 sectors 2146765824 bytes
9 008401932 sectors 4301789184 bytes
11 010490382 sectors 5371075584 bytes
13 004208967 sectors 2154991104 bytes
15 027712062 sectors 14188575744 bytes</pre> Partition Hashes 43F12 md5sum 16418304 CBA0C9984F51778E89DEF0C6BED06864 43F16 md5sum 1077479424 37E81FFB31C3CB38AA48B2237500908E 43F32 md5sum 4301789184 2C4D8D450E5AD28329F616D87114CCFE 43F32x md5sum 10742183424 5980CB0FA68E9862C65765DF50F00906 43swap md5sum 2154991104 4B602964A30FE20D1B22B046A7375A7C 43x2 md5sum 5371075584 C7A84DE9ACBCB05463604CE8823D0874 43NTFS md5sum 14188575744 5D42FA317C802ACFEF2D313092D7411E
Log	Actual Date:01/05/07 02:52:32PM

```
Test Case DA-06-ATA28 Linen 5.05f
Highlights:   File Integrity:Completely Verified, 0 Errors
              Acquisition Hash:bc39c3f7ee7a50e77b9ba1e65a5aeef7
              Verify Hash:bc39c3f7ee7a50e77b9ba1e65a5aeef7
              EnCase Version:5.05f
              System Version:Linux
              Error Granularity:64
              Total Size:40,000,000,000 bytes (37.3GB)
              Total Sectors:78,125,000

              Rehash of Source MD5: BC39C3F7EE7A50E77B9BA1E65A5AEEF7
```

Results:

Assertion & Expected Result	Actual Result
AM-01 Source acquired using interface AI.	as expected
AM-02 Source is type DS.	as expected
AM-03 Execution environment is XE.	as expected
AM-05 An image is created on file system type FS.	as expected
AM-06 All visible sectors acquired.	as expected
AM-08 All sectors accurately acquired.	as expected
AO-01 Image file is complete and accurate.	as expected
AO-05 Multifile image created.	as expected
AO-22 Tool calculates hashes by block.	option not available
AO-23 Logged information is correct.	as expected
AO-24 Source is unchanged by acquisition.	as expected

Analysis: Expected results achieved

5.2.2 DA-06-ATA48

Test Case DA-06-ATA48 Linen 5.05f	
Case Summary:	DA-06 Acquire a physical device using access interface AI to an image file.
Assertions:	AM-01 The tool uses access interface SRC-AI to access the digital source. AM-02 The tool acquires digital source DS. AM-03 The tool executes in execution environment XE. AM-05 If image file creation is specified, the tool creates an image file on file system type FS. AM-06 All visible sectors are acquired from the digital source. AM-08 All sectors acquired from the digital source are acquired accurately. AO-01 If the tool creates an image file, the data represented by the image file is the same as the data acquired by the tool. AO-05 If the tool creates a multi-file image of a requested size then all the individual files shall be no larger than the requested size. AO-22 If requested, the tool calculates block hashes for a specified block size during an acquisition for each block acquired from the digital source. AO-23 If the tool logs any log significant information, the information is accurately recorded in the log file. AO-24 If the tool executes in a forensically safe execution environment, the digital source is unchanged by the acquisition process.
Tester Name:	brl
Test Host:	Max
Test Date:	Wed Jan 24 16:56:08 2007
Drives:	src(4C) dst (none) other (28-IDE)
Source Setup:	src hash (SHA1): < 8FF620D2BEDCCAFE8412EDAAD56C8554F872EFBF > src hash (MD5): < D10F763B56D4CEBA2D1311C61F9FB382 > 390721968 total sectors (200049647616 bytes) 24320/254/63 (max cyl/hd values) 24321/255/63 (number of cyl/hd) IDE disk: Model (WDC WD2000JB-00KFA0) serial # (WD-WMAMR1031111) N Start LBA Length Start C/H/S End C/H/S boot Partition type 1 P 000000063 390700737 0000/001/01 1023/254/63 Boot 07 NTFS 2 P 000000000 000000000 0000/000/00 0000/000/00 00 empty entry 3 P 000000000 000000000 0000/000/00 0000/000/00 00 empty entry 4 P 000000000 000000000 0000/000/00 0000/000/00 00 empty entry 1 390700737 sectors 200038777344 bytes
Log Highlights:	Actual Date:01/24/07 05:27:21PM File Integrity:Completely Verified, 0 Errors Acquisition Hash:d10f763b56d4ceba2d1311c61f9fb382 Verify Hash:d10f763b56d4ceba2d1311c61f9fb382 EnCase Version:5.05f System Version:Linux Error Granularity:64 Total Size:200,049,647,616 bytes (186.3GB) Total Sectors:390,721,968 Rehash of Source MD5: D10F763B56D4CEBA2D1311C61F9FB382
Results:	

Assertion & Expected Result	Actual Result
AM-01 Source acquired using interface AI.	as expected
AM-02 Source is type DS.	as expected
AM-03 Execution environment is XE.	as expected
AM-05 An image is created on file system type FS.	as expected
AM-06 All visible sectors acquired.	as expected
AM-08 All sectors accurately acquired.	as expected
AO-01 Image file is complete and accurate.	as expected
AO-05 Multifile image created.	as expected
AO-22 Tool calculates hashes by block.	option not available
AO-23 Logged information is correct.	as expected
AO-24 Source is unchanged by acquisition.	as expected

Analysis:	Expected results achieved

5.2.3 DA-06-FIRE

Test Case DA-06-FIRE Linen 5.05f	
Case Summary:	DA-06 Acquire a physical device using access interface AI to an image file.
Assertions:	AM-01 The tool uses access interface SRC-AI to access the digital source. AM-02 The tool acquires digital source DS. AM-03 The tool executes in execution environment XE. AM-05 If image file creation is specified, the tool creates an image file on file system type FS. AM-06 All visible sectors are acquired from the digital source. AM-08 All sectors acquired from the digital source are acquired accurately. AO-01 If the tool creates an image file, the data represented by the image file is the same as the data acquired by the tool. AO-05 If the tool creates a multi-file image of a requested size then all the individual files shall be no larger than the requested size. AO-22 If requested, the tool calculates block hashes for a specified block size during an acquisition for each block acquired from the digital source. AO-23 If the tool logs any log significant information, the information is accurately recorded in the log file. AO-24 If the tool executes in a forensically safe execution environment, the digital source is unchanged by the acquisition process.
Tester Name:	brl
Test Host:	AndWife
Test Date:	Tue Jan 16 11:35:41 2007
Drives:	src(63-FU2) dst (none) other (EF)
Source Setup:	src hash (SHA1): < F7069EDCBEAC863C88DECED82159F22DA96BE99B > src hash (MD5): < EE217BC4FA4F3D1B4021D29B065AA9EC > 117304992 total sectors (60060155904 bytes) Model (SP0612N) serial # () N Start LBA Length Start C/H/S End C/H/S boot Partition type 1 P 000000063 004192902 0000/001/01 0260/254/63 Boot 06 Fat16 2 X 004192965 113097600 0261/000/01 1023/254/63 0F extended 3 S 000000063 113097537 0261/001/01 1023/254/63 0B Fat32 4 S 000000000 000000000 0000/000/00 0000/000/00 00 empty entry 5 P 000000000 000000000 0000/000/00 0000/000/00 00 empty entry 6 P 000000000 000000000 0000/000/00 0000/000/00 00 empty entry 1 004192902 sectors 2146765824 bytes 3 113097537 sectors 57905938944 bytes
Log Highlights:	Actual Date:01/16/07 01:57:57PM File Integrity:Completely Verified, 0 Errors Acquisition Hash:ee217bc4fa4f3d1b4021d29b065aa9ec Verify Hash:ee217bc4fa4f3d1b4021d29b065aa9ec EnCase Version:5.05f System Version:Linux Error Granularity:64 Total Size:60,060,155,904 bytes (55.9GB) Total Sectors:117,304,992 Rehash of Source MD5: EE217BC4FA4F3D1B4021D29B065AA9EC
Results:	

Assertion & Expected Result	Actual Result
AM-01 Source acquired using interface AI.	as expected
AM-02 Source is type DS.	as expected
AM-03 Execution environment is XE.	as expected
AM-05 An image is created on file system type FS.	as expected
AM-06 All visible sectors acquired.	as expected
AM-08 All sectors accurately acquired.	as expected
AO-01 Image file is complete and accurate.	as expected
AO-05 Multifile image created.	as expected
AO-22 Tool calculates hashes by block.	option not available
AO-23 Logged information is correct.	as expected
AO-24 Source is unchanged by acquisition.	as expected

Test Case DA-06-FIRE Linen 5.05f	
Analysis:	Expected results achieved

5.2.4 DA-06-SATA28

Test Case DA-06-SATA28 Linen 5.05f	
Case Summary:	DA-06 Acquire a physical device using access interface AI to an image file.
Assertions:	AM-01 The tool uses access interface SRC-AI to access the digital source.
	AM-02 The tool acquires digital source DS.
	AM-03 The tool executes in execution environment XE.
	AM-05 If image file creation is specified, the tool creates an image file on file system type FS.
	AM-06 All visible sectors are acquired from the digital source.
	AM-08 All sectors acquired from the digital source are acquired accurately.
	AO-01 If the tool creates an image file, the data represented by the image file is the same as the data acquired by the tool.
	AO-05 If the tool creates a multi-file image of a requested size then all the individual files shall be no larger than the requested size.
	AO-22 If requested, the tool calculates block hashes for a specified block size during an acquisition for each block acquired from the digital source.
	AO-23 If the tool logs any log significant information, the information is accurately recorded in the log file.
	AO-24 If the tool executes in a forensically safe execution environment, the digital source is unchanged by the acquisition process.
Tester Name:	brl
Test Host:	Max
Test Date:	Wed Jan 17 14:17:03 2007
Drives:	src(07) dst (none) other (EF)
Source Setup:	src hash (SHA1): < 655E9BDDB36A3F9C5C4CC8BF32B8C5B41AF9F52E >
	src hash (MD5): < 2EAF712DAD80F66E30DEA00365B4579B >
	156301488 total sectors (80026361856 bytes)
	Model (WDC WD800JD-32HK) serial # (WD-WMAJ91510044)
	N Start LBA Length Start C/H/S End C/H/S boot Partition type
	1 P 000000063 156280257 0000/001/01 1023/254/63 Boot 07 NTFS
	2 P 000000000 000000000 0000/000/00 0000/000/00 00 empty entry
	3 P 000000000 000000000 0000/000/00 0000/000/00 00 empty entry
	4 P 000000000 000000000 0000/000/00 0000/000/00 00 empty entry
	1 156280257 sectors 80015491584 bytes
Log Highlights:	Actual Date:01/17/07 02:26:24PM
	File Integrity:Completely Verified, 0 Errors
	Acquisition Hash:2eaf712dad80f66e30dea00365b4579b
	Verify Hash:2eaf712dad80f66e30dea00365b4579b
	EnCase Version:5.05f
	System Version:Linux
	Error Granularity:64
	Total Size:80,026,361,856 bytes (74.5GB)
	Total Sectors:156,301,488
	Rehash of Source MD5: 2EAF712DAD80F66E30DEA00365B4579B

Results:		
	Assertion & Expected Result	**Actual Result**
	AM-01 Source acquired using interface AI.	as expected
	AM-02 Source is type DS.	as expected
	AM-03 Execution environment is XE.	as expected
	AM-05 An image is created on file system type FS.	as expected
	AM-06 All visible sectors acquired.	as expected
	AM-08 All sectors accurately acquired.	as expected
	AO-01 Image file is complete and accurate.	as expected
	AO-05 Multifile image created.	as expected
	AO-22 Tool calculates hashes by block.	option not available
	AO-23 Logged information is correct.	as expected
	AO-24 Source is unchanged by acquisition.	as expected

Analysis:	Expected results achieved

5.2.5 DA-06-SATA48

Test Case DA-06-SATA48 Linen 5.05f	
Case Summary:	DA-06 Acquire a physical device using access interface AI to an image file.
Assertions:	AM-01 The tool uses access interface SRC-AI to access the digital source. AM-02 The tool acquires digital source DS. AM-03 The tool executes in execution environment XE. AM-05 If image file creation is specified, the tool creates an image file on file system type FS. AM-06 All visible sectors are acquired from the digital source. AM-08 All sectors acquired from the digital source are acquired accurately. AO-01 If the tool creates an image file, the data represented by the image file is the same as the data acquired by the tool. AO-05 If the tool creates a multi-file image of a requested size then all the individual files shall be no larger than the requested size. AO-22 If requested, the tool calculates block hashes for a specified block size during an acquisition for each block acquired from the digital source. AO-23 If the tool logs any log significant information, the information is accurately recorded in the log file. AO-24 If the tool executes in a forensically safe execution environment, the digital source is unchanged by the acquisition process.
Tester Name:	brl
Test Host:	Max
Test Date:	Tue Jan 16 16:51:34 2007
Drives:	src(0D) dst (none) other (EF)
Source Setup:	src hash (SHA1): < BAAD80E8781E55F2E3EF528CA73BD41D228C1377 > src hash (MD5): < 1FA7C3CBE60EB9E89863DED2411E40C9 > 488397168 total sectors (250059350016 bytes) 30400/254/63 (max cyl/hd values) 30401/255/63 (number of cyl/hd) Model (WDC WD2500JD-22F) serial # (WD-WMAEH2678216) N Start LBA Length Start C/H/S End C/H/S boot Partition type 1 P 000000063 488375937 0000/001/01 1023/254/63 Boot 07 NTFS 2 P 000000000 000000000 0000/000/00 0000/000/00 00 empty entry 3 P 000000000 000000000 0000/000/00 0000/000/00 00 empty entry 4 P 000000000 000000000 0000/000/00 0000/000/00 00 empty entry 1 488375937 sectors 250048479744 bytes
Log Highlights:	Actual Date:01/16/07 05:13:52PM File Integrity:Completely Verified, 0 Errors Acquisition Hash:1fa7c3cbe60eb9e89863ded2411e40c9 Verify Hash:1fa7c3cbe60eb9e89863ded2411e40c9 EnCase Version:5.05f System Version:Linux Error Granularity:64 Total Size:250,059,350,016 bytes (232.9GB) Total Sectors:488,397,168 Rehash of Source MD5: 1FA7C3CBE60EB9E89863DED2411E40C9
Results:	

Assertion & Expected Result	Actual Result
AM-01 Source acquired using interface AI.	as expected
AM-02 Source is type DS.	as expected
AM-03 Execution environment is XE.	as expected
AM-05 An image is created on file system type FS.	as expected
AM-06 All visible sectors acquired.	as expected
AM-08 All sectors accurately acquired.	as expected
AO-01 Image file is complete and accurate.	as expected
AO-05 Multifile image created.	as expected
AO-22 Tool calculates hashes by block.	option not available
AO-23 Logged information is correct.	as expected
AO-24 Source is unchanged by acquisition.	as expected

Analysis:	Expected results achieved

5.2.6 DA-06-SCSI

Test Case DA-06-SCSI Linen 5.05f	
Case Summary:	DA-06 Acquire a physical device using access interface AI to an image file.
Assertions:	AM-01 The tool uses access interface SRC-AI to access the digital source. AM-02 The tool acquires digital source DS. AM-03 The tool executes in execution environment XE. AM-05 If image file creation is specified, the tool creates an image file on file system type FS. AM-06 All visible sectors are acquired from the digital source. AM-08 All sectors acquired from the digital source are acquired accurately. AO-01 If the tool creates an image file, the data represented by the image file is the same as the data acquired by the tool. AO-05 If the tool creates a multi-file image of a requested size then all the individual files shall be no larger than the requested size. AO-22 If requested, the tool calculates block hashes for a specified block size during an acquisition for each block acquired from the digital source. AO-23 If the tool logs any log significant information, the information is accurately recorded in the log file. AO-24 If the tool executes in a forensically safe execution environment, the digital source is unchanged by the acquisition process.
Tester Name:	brl
Test Host:	Max
Test Date:	Wed Jan 10 15:22:26 2007
Drives:	src(2A) dst (none) other (EF)
Source Setup:	src hash (SHA1): < F5F9F2903DCAB895F36E270FB22A722E27918125 > src hash (MD5): < 91E0AC905F682ECF6DE4E9835089B519 > 17783249 total sectors (9105023488 bytes) Model (QM39100TD-SCA) serial # (PCB=20-116711-06 HDAQM39100TD-SCA) N Start LBA Length Start C/H/S End C/H/S boot Partition type 1 P 000000063 017751762 0000/001/01 1023/254/63 Boot 07 NTFS 2 P 000000000 000000000 0000/000/00 0000/000/00 00 empty entry 3 P 000000000 000000000 0000/000/00 0000/000/00 00 empty entry 4 P 000000000 000000000 0000/000/00 0000/000/00 00 empty entry 1 017751762 sectors 9088902144 bytes
Log Highlights:	Actual Date:01/12/07 05:48:38PM File Integrity:Completely Verified, 0 Errors Acquisition Hash:91e0ac905f682ecf6de4e9835089b519 Verify Hash:91e0ac905f682ecf6de4e9835089b519 EnCase Version:5.05f System Version:Linux Error Granularity:64 Total Size:9,105,023,488 bytes (8.5GB) Total Sectors:17,783,249 Rehash of Source MD5: 91E0AC905F682ECF6DE4E9835089B519
Results:	

Assertion & Expected Result	Actual Result
AM-01 Source acquired using interface AI.	as expected
AM-02 Source is type DS.	as expected
AM-03 Execution environment is XE.	as expected
AM-05 An image is created on file system type FS.	as expected
AM-06 All visible sectors acquired.	as expected
AM-08 All sectors accurately acquired.	as expected
AO-01 Image file is complete and accurate.	as expected
AO-05 Multifile image created.	as expected
AO-22 Tool calculates hashes by block.	option not available
AO-23 Logged information is correct.	as expected
AO-24 Source is unchanged by acquisition.	as expected

Analysis:	Expected results achieved

5.2.7 DA-06-USB

Test Case DA-06-USB Linen 5.05f	
Case Summary:	DA-06 Acquire a physical device using access interface AI to an image file.
Assertions:	AM-01 The tool uses access interface SRC-AI to access the digital source. AM-02 The tool acquires digital source DS. AM-03 The tool executes in execution environment XE. AM-05 If image file creation is specified, the tool creates an image file on file system type FS. AM-06 All visible sectors are acquired from the digital source. AM-08 All sectors acquired from the digital source are acquired accurately. AO-01 If the tool creates an image file, the data represented by the image file is the same as the data acquired by the tool. AO-05 If the tool creates a multi-file image of a requested size then all the individual files shall be no larger than the requested size. AO-22 If requested, the tool calculates block hashes for a specified block size during an acquisition for each block acquired from the digital source. AO-23 If the tool logs any log significant information, the information is accurately recorded in the log file. AO-24 If the tool executes in a forensically safe execution environment, the digital source is unchanged by the acquisition process.
Tester Name:	brl
Test Host:	AndWife
Test Date:	Wed Jan 24 13:58:01 2007
Drives:	src(63-FU2) dst (none) other (EF)
Source Setup:	src hash (SHA1): < F7069EDCBEAC863C88DECED82159F22DA96BE99B > src hash (MD5): < EE217BC4FA4F3D1B4021D29B065AA9EC > 117304992 total sectors (60060155904 bytes) Model (SP0612N) serial # () N Start LBA Length Start C/H/S End C/H/S boot Partition type 1 P 000000063 004192902 0000/001/01 0260/254/63 Boot 06 Fat16 2 X 004192965 113097600 0261/000/01 1023/254/63 0F extended 3 S 000000063 113097537 0261/001/01 1023/254/63 0B Fat32 4 S 000000000 000000000 0000/000/00 0000/000/00 00 empty entry 5 P 000000000 000000000 0000/000/00 0000/000/00 00 empty entry 6 P 000000000 000000000 0000/000/00 0000/000/00 00 empty entry 1 004192902 sectors 2146765824 bytes 3 113097537 sectors 57905938944 bytes
Log Highlights:	Actual Date:01/24/07 02:08:31PM File Integrity:Completely Verified, 0 Errors Acquisition Hash:ee217bc4fa4f3d1b4021d29b065aa9ec Verify Hash:ee217bc4fa4f3d1b4021d29b065aa9ec EnCase Version:5.05f System Version:Linux Error Granularity:64 Total Size:60,060,155,904 bytes (55.9GB) Total Sectors:117,304,992 Rehash of Source MD5: EE217BC4FA4F3D1B4021D29B065AA9EC
Results:	

Assertion & Expected Result	Actual Result
AM-01 Source acquired using interface AI.	as expected
AM-02 Source is type DS.	as expected
AM-03 Execution environment is XE.	as expected
AM-05 An image is created on file system type FS.	as expected
AM-06 All visible sectors acquired.	as expected
AM-08 All sectors accurately acquired.	as expected
AO-01 Image file is complete and accurate.	as expected
AO-05 Multifile image created.	as expected
AO-22 Tool calculates hashes by block.	option not available
AO-23 Logged information is correct.	as expected
AO-24 Source is unchanged by acquisition.	as expected

Test Case DA-06-USB Linen 5.05f	
Analysis:	Expected results achieved

5.2.8 DA-07-NT

Test Case DA-07-NT Linen 5.05f	
Case Summary:	DA-07 Acquire a digital source of type DS to an image file.
Assertions:	AM-01 The tool uses access interface SRC-AI to access the digital source. AM-02 The tool acquires digital source DS. AM-03 The tool executes in execution environment XE. AM-05 If image file creation is specified, the tool creates an image file on file system type FS. AM-06 All visible sectors are acquired from the digital source. AM-08 All sectors acquired from the digital source are acquired accurately. AO-01 If the tool creates an image file, the data represented by the image file is the same as the data acquired by the tool. AO-05 If the tool creates a multi-file image of a requested size then all the individual files shall be no larger than the requested size. AO-22 If requested, the tool calculates block hashes for a specified block size during an acquisition for each block acquired from the digital source. AO-23 If the tool logs any log significant information, the information is accurately recorded in the log file. AO-24 If the tool executes in a forensically safe execution environment, the digital source is unchanged by the acquisition process.
Tester Name:	brl
Test Host:	AndWife
Test Date:	Wed Feb 7 16:30:39 2007
Drives:	src(43) dst (none) other (EF)
Source Setup:	src hash (SHA1): < 888E2E7F7AD237DC7A732281DD93F325065E5871 > src hash (MD5): < BC39C3F7EE7A50E77B9BA1E65A5AEEF7 > 78125000 total sectors (40000000000 bytes) Model (0BB-75JHC0) serial # (WD-WMAMC46588) 　N　Start LBA Length 　　Start C/H/S End C/H/S 　boot Partition type 　1 P 000000063 020980827 0000/001/01 1023/254/63 　　0C Fat32X 　2 X 020980890 057143205 1023/000/01 1023/254/63 　　0F extended 　3 S 000000063 000032067 1023/001/01 1023/254/63 　　01 Fat12 　4 x 000032130 002104515 1023/000/01 1023/254/63 　　05 extended 　5 S 000000063 002104452 1023/001/01 1023/254/63 　　06 Fat16 　6 x 002136645 004192965 1023/000/01 1023/254/63 　　05 extended 　7 S 000000063 004192902 1023/001/01 1023/254/63 　　16 other 　8 x 006329610 008401995 1023/000/01 1023/254/63 　　05 extended 　9 S 000000063 008401932 1023/001/01 1023/254/63 　　0B Fat32 10 x 014731605 010490445 1023/000/01 1023/254/63 　　05 extended 11 S 000000063 010490382 1023/001/01 1023/254/63 　　83 Linux 12 x 025222050 004209030 1023/000/01 1023/254/63 　　05 extended 13 S 000000063 004208967 1023/001/01 1023/254/63 　　82 Linux swap 14 x 029431080 027712125 1023/000/01 1023/254/63 　　05 extended 15 S 000000063 027712062 1023/001/01 1023/254/63 　　07 NTFS 16 S 000000000 000000000 0000/000/00 0000/000/00 　　00 empty entry 17 P 000000000 000000000 0000/000/00 0000/000/00 　　00 empty entry 18 P 000000000 000000000 0000/000/00 0000/000/00 　　00 empty entry 1 020980827 sectors 10742183424 bytes 3 000032067 sectors 16418304 bytes 5 002104452 sectors 1077479424 bytes 7 004192902 sectors 2146765824 bytes 9 008401932 sectors 4301789184 bytes 11 010490382 sectors 5371075584 bytes 13 004208967 sectors 2154991104 bytes 15 027712062 sectors 14188575744 bytes Partition Hashes 43F12 md5sum 16418304 CBA0C9984F51778E89DEF0C6BED06864 43F16 md5sum 1077479424 37E81FFB31C3CB38AA48B2237500908E 43F32 md5sum 4301789184 2C4D8D450E5AD28329F616D87114CCFE 43F32x md5sum 10742183424 5980CB0FA68E9862C65765DF50F00906 43swap md5sum 2154991104 4B602964A30FE20D1B22B046A7375A7C 43x2 md5sum 5371075584 C7A84DE9ACBCB05463604CE8823D0874 43NTFS md5sum 14188575744 5D42FA317C802ACFEF2D313092D7411E
Log	Total Capacity:14,188,572,672 bytes (13.2GB)

Test Case DA-07-NT Linen 5.05f	
Highlights:	Total Clusters:3,464,007Unallocated:14,118,940,672 bytes (13.1GB) Actual Date:02/07/07 04:36:33PM File Integrity:Completely Verified, 0 Errors Acquisition Hash:5d42fa317c802acfef2d313092d7411e Verify Hash:5d42fa317c802acfef2d313092d7411e EnCase Version:5.05f System Version:Linux Error Granularity:64 Total Size:14,188,575,744 bytes (13.2GB) Total Sectors:27,712,062 Rehash of Source MD5: BC39C3F7EE7A50E77B9BA1E65A5AEEF7
Results:	

Assertion & Expected Result	Actual Result
AM-01 Source acquired using interface AI.	as expected
AM-02 Source is type DS.	as expected
AM-03 Execution environment is XE.	as expected
AM-05 An image is created on file system type FS.	as expected
AM-06 All visible sectors acquired.	as expected
AM-08 All sectors accurately acquired.	as expected
AO-01 Image file is complete and accurate.	as expected
AO-05 Multifile image created.	as expected
AO-22 Tool calculates hashes by block.	option not available
AO-23 Logged information is correct.	as expected
AO-24 Source is unchanged by acquisition.	as expected

Analysis:	Expected results achieved

5.2.9 DA-07-CF

Test Case DA-07-CF Linen 5.05f	
Case Summary:	DA-07 Acquire a digital source of type DS to an image file.
Assertions:	AM-01 The tool uses access interface SRC-AI to access the digital source. AM-02 The tool acquires digital source DS. AM-03 The tool executes in execution environment XE. AM-05 If image file creation is specified, the tool creates an image file on file system type FS. AM-06 All visible sectors are acquired from the digital source. AM-08 All sectors acquired from the digital source are acquired accurately. AO-01 If the tool creates an image file, the data represented by the image file is the same as the data acquired by the tool. AO-05 If the tool creates a multi-file image of a requested size then all the individual files shall be no larger than the requested size. AO-22 If requested, the tool calculates block hashes for a specified block size during an acquisition for each block acquired from the digital source. AO-23 If the tool logs any log significant information, the information is accurately recorded in the log file. AO-24 If the tool executes in a forensically safe execution environment, the digital source is unchanged by the acquisition process.
Tester Name:	brl
Test Host:	AndWife
Test Date:	Tue Feb 6 16:22:18 2007
Drives:	src(C1-CF) dst (none) other (52-IDE)
Source Setup:	src hash (SHA1): < 5B8235178DF99FA307430C088F81746606638A0B > src hash (MD5): < 776DF8B4D2589E21DEBCF589EDC16D78 > 503808 total sectors (257949696 bytes) Model (CF) serial # () N Start LBA Length Start C/H/S End C/H/S boot Partition type 1 P 778135908 1141509631 0357/116/40 0357/032/45 Boot 72 other 2 P 168689522 1936028240 0288/115/43 0367/114/50 Boot 65 other 3 P 1869881465 1936028192 0366/032/33 0357/032/43 Boot 79 other 4 P 2885681152 000055499 0372/097/50 0000/010/00 Boot 0D other 1 1141509631 sectors 584452931072 bytes 2 1936028240 sectors 991246458880 bytes 3 1936028192 sectors 991246434304 bytes 4 000055499 sectors 28415488 bytes
Log Highlights:	Actual Date:02/06/07 04:29:07PM File Integrity:Completely Verified, 0 Errors Acquisition Hash:776df8b4d2589e21debcf589edc16d78 Verify Hash:776df8b4d2589e21debcf589edc16d78 EnCase Version:5.05f System Version:Linux Error Granularity:64 Total Size:257,949,696 bytes (246MB) Total Sectors:503,808 Rehash of Source MD5: 776DF8B4D2589E21DEBCF589EDC16D78
Results:	

Assertion & Expected Result	Actual Result
AM-01 Source acquired using interface AI.	as expected
AM-02 Source is type DS.	as expected
AM-03 Execution environment is XE.	as expected
AM-05 An image is created on file system type FS.	as expected
AM-06 All visible sectors acquired.	as expected
AM-08 All sectors accurately acquired.	as expected
AO-01 Image file is complete and accurate.	as expected
AO-05 Multifile image created.	as expected
AO-22 Tool calculates hashes by block.	option not available
AO-23 Logged information is correct.	as expected
AO-24 Source is unchanged by acquisition.	as expected

Test Case DA-07-CF Linen 5.05f	
Analysis:	Expected results achieved

5.2.10   DA-07-F12

Test Case DA-07-F12 Linen 5.05f	
Case Summary:	DA-07 Acquire a digital source of type DS to an image file.
Assertions:	AM-01 The tool uses access interface SRC-AI to access the digital source. AM-02 The tool acquires digital source DS. AM-03 The tool executes in execution environment XE. AM-05 If image file creation is specified, the tool creates an image file on file system type FS. AM-06 All visible sectors are acquired from the digital source. AM-08 All sectors acquired from the digital source are acquired accurately. AO-01 If the tool creates an image file, the data represented by the image file is the same as the data acquired by the tool. AO-05 If the tool creates a multi-file image of a requested size then all the individual files shall be no larger than the requested size. AO-22 If requested, the tool calculates block hashes for a specified block size during an acquisition for each block acquired from the digital source. AO-23 If the tool logs any log significant information, the information is accurately recorded in the log file. AO-24 If the tool executes in a forensically safe execution environment, the digital source is unchanged by the acquisition process.
Tester Name:	brl
Test Host:	AndWife
Test Date:	Wed Feb 7 14:21:01 2007
Drives:	src(43) dst (none) other (EF)

Source Setup:	src hash (SHA1): < 888E2E7F7AD237DC7A732281DD93F325065E5871 >
	src hash (MD5): < BC39C3F7EE7A50E77B9BA1E65A5AEEF7 >
	78125000 total sectors (40000000000 bytes)
	Model (0BB-75JHC0) serial # (WD-WMAMC46588)
	<pre>N Start LBA Length Start C/H/S End C/H/S boot Partition type
	 1 P 000000063 020980827 0000/001/01 1023/254/63 0C Fat32X
	 2 X 020980890 057143205 1023/000/01 1023/254/63 0F extended
	 3 S 000000063 000032067 1023/001/01 1023/254/63 01 Fat12
	 4 x 000032130 002104515 1023/000/01 1023/254/63 05 extended
	 5 S 000000063 002104452 1023/001/01 1023/254/63 06 Fat16
	 6 x 002136645 004192965 1023/000/01 1023/254/63 05 extended
	 7 S 000000063 004192902 1023/001/01 1023/254/63 16 other
	 8 x 006329610 008401995 1023/000/01 1023/254/63 05 extended
	 9 S 000000063 008401932 1023/001/01 1023/254/63 0B Fat32
	10 x 014731605 010490445 1023/000/01 1023/254/63 05 extended
	11 S 000000063 010490382 1023/001/01 1023/254/63 83 Linux
	12 x 025222050 004209030 1023/000/01 1023/254/63 05 extended
	13 S 000000063 004208967 1023/001/01 1023/254/63 82 Linux swap
	14 x 029431080 027712125 1023/000/01 1023/254/63 05 extended
	15 S 000000063 027712062 1023/001/01 1023/254/63 07 NTFS
	16 S 000000000 000000000 0000/000/00 0000/000/00 00 empty entry
	17 P 000000000 000000000 0000/000/00 0000/000/00 00 empty entry
	18 P 000000000 000000000 0000/000/00 0000/000/00 00 empty entry
	 1 020980827 sectors 10742183424 bytes
	 3 000032067 sectors 16418304 bytes
	 5 002104452 sectors 1077479424 bytes
	 7 004192902 sectors 2146765824 bytes
	 9 008401932 sectors 4301789184 bytes
	11 010490382 sectors 5371075584 bytes
	13 004208967 sectors 2154991104 bytes
	15 027712062 sectors 14188575744 bytes
	
	Partition Hashes
	43F12 md5sum 16418304 CBA0C9984F51778E89DEF0C6BED06864
	43F16 md5sum 1077479424 37E81FFB31C3CB38AA48B2237500908E
	43F32 md5sum 4301789184 2C4D8D450E5AD28329F616D87114CCFE
	43F32x md5sum 10742183424 5980CB0FA68E9862C65765DF50F00906
	43swap md5sum 2154991104 4B602964A30FE20D1B22B046A7375A7C
	43x2 md5sum 5371075584 C7A84DE9ACBCB05463604CE8823D0874
	43NTFS md5sum 14188575744 5D42FA317C802ACFEF2D313092D7411E</pre>

Log	Total Capacity:16,384,000 bytes (15.6MB)

Test Case DA-07-F12 Linen 5.05f	
Highlights:	Total Clusters:4,000Unallocated:15,208,448 bytes (14.5MB) OEM Version:MSWIN4.0Serial Number:888A-2896 Actual Date:02/07/07 02:26:56PM File Integrity:Completely Verified, 0 Errors Acquisition Hash:cba0c9984f51778e89def0c6bed06864 Verify Hash:cba0c9984f51778e89def0c6bed06864 EnCase Version:5.05f System Version:Linux Error Granularity:64 Total Size:16,418,304 bytes (15.7MB) Total Sectors:32,067 Rehash of Source MD5: BC39C3F7EE7A50E77B9BA1E65A5AEEF7
Results:	

Assertion & Expected Result	Actual Result
AM-01 Source acquired using interface AI.	as expected
AM-02 Source is type DS.	as expected
AM-03 Execution environment is XE.	as expected
AM-05 An image is created on file system type FS.	as expected
AM-06 All visible sectors acquired.	as expected
AM-08 All sectors accurately acquired.	as expected
AO-01 Image file is complete and accurate.	as expected
AO-05 Multifile image created.	as expected
AO-22 Tool calculates hashes by block.	option not available
AO-23 Logged information is correct.	as expected
AO-24 Source is unchanged by acquisition.	as expected

Analysis:	Expected results achieved

5.2.11 DA-07-F16

Test Case DA-07-F16 Linen 5.05f	
Case Summary:	DA-07 Acquire a digital source of type DS to an image file.
Assertions:	AM-01 The tool uses access interface SRC-AI to access the digital source. AM-02 The tool acquires digital source DS. AM-03 The tool executes in execution environment XE. AM-05 If image file creation is specified, the tool creates an image file on file system type FS. AM-06 All visible sectors are acquired from the digital source. AM-08 All sectors acquired from the digital source are acquired accurately. AO-01 If the tool creates an image file, the data represented by the image file is the same as the data acquired by the tool. AO-05 If the tool creates a multi-file image of a requested size then all the individual files shall be no larger than the requested size. AO-22 If requested, the tool calculates block hashes for a specified block size during an acquisition for each block acquired from the digital source. AO-23 If the tool logs any log significant information, the information is accurately recorded in the log file. AO-24 If the tool executes in a forensically safe execution environment, the digital source is unchanged by the acquisition process.
Tester Name:	brl
Test Host:	AndWife
Test Date:	Wed Feb 7 15:13:42 2007
Drives:	src(43) dst (none) other (EF)

Source Setup:	src hash (SHA1): < 888E2E7F7AD237DC7A732281DD93F325065E5871 >
	src hash (MD5): < BC39C3F7EE7A50E77B9BA1E65A5AEEF7 >
	78125000 total sectors (40000000000 bytes)
	Model (0BB-75JHC0) serial # (WD-WMAMC46588)
	<pre>N Start LBA Length Start C/H/S End C/H/S boot Partition type
	 1 P 000000063 020980827 0000/001/01 1023/254/63 0C Fat32X
	 2 X 020980890 057143205 1023/000/01 1023/254/63 0F extended
	 3 S 000000063 000032067 1023/001/01 1023/254/63 01 Fat12
	 4 x 000032130 002104515 1023/000/01 1023/254/63 05 extended
	 5 S 000000063 002104452 1023/001/01 1023/254/63 06 Fat16
	 6 x 002136645 004192965 1023/000/01 1023/254/63 05 extended
	 7 S 000000063 004192902 1023/001/01 1023/254/63 16 other
	 8 x 006329610 008401995 1023/000/01 1023/254/63 05 extended
	 9 S 000000063 008401932 1023/001/01 1023/254/63 0B Fat32
	10 x 014731605 010490445 1023/000/01 1023/254/63 05 extended
	11 S 000000063 010490382 1023/001/01 1023/254/63 83 Linux
	12 x 025222050 004209030 1023/000/01 1023/254/63 05 extended
	13 S 000000063 004208967 1023/001/01 1023/254/63 82 Linux swap
	14 x 029431080 027712125 1023/000/01 1023/254/63 05 extended
	15 S 000000063 027712062 1023/001/01 1023/254/63 07 NTFS
	16 S 000000000 000000000 0000/000/00 0000/000/00 00 empty entry
	17 P 000000000 000000000 0000/000/00 0000/000/00 00 empty entry
	18 P 000000000 000000000 0000/000/00 0000/000/00 00 empty entry
	1 020980827 sectors 10742183424 bytes
	3 000032067 sectors 16418304 bytes
	5 002104452 sectors 1077479424 bytes
	7 004192902 sectors 2146765824 bytes
	9 008401932 sectors 4301789184 bytes
	11 010490382 sectors 5371075584 bytes
	13 004208967 sectors 2154991104 bytes
	15 027712062 sectors 14188575744 bytes
	
	Partition Hashes
	43F12 md5sum 16418304 CBA0C9984F51778E89DEF0C6BED06864
	43F16 md5sum 1077479424 37E81FFB31C3CB38AA48B2237500908E
	43F32 md5sum 4301789184 2C4D8D450E5AD28329F616D87114CCFE
	43F32x md5sum 10742183424 5980CB0FA68E9862C65765DF50F00906
	43swap md5sum 2154991104 4B602964A30FE20D1B22B046A7375A7C
	43x2 md5sum 5371075584 C7A84DE9ACBCB05463604CE8823D0874
	43NTFS md5sum 14188575744 5D42FA317C802ACFEF2D313092D7411E</pre>

Log	Total Capacity:1,077,313,536 bytes (1GB)

Test Case DA-07-F16 Linen 5.05f	
Highlights:	Total Clusters:32,877Unallocated:1,076,953,088 bytes (1GB) OEM Version:MSWIN4.0Serial Number:CCCF-3DAD Actual Date:02/07/07 03:18:50PM File Integrity:Completely Verified, 0 Errors Acquisition Hash:37e81ffb31c3cb38aa48b2237500908e Verify Hash:37e81ffb31c3cb38aa48b2237500908e EnCase Version:5.05f System Version:Linux Error Granularity:64 Total Size:1,077,479,424 bytes (1GB) Total Sectors:2,104,452 Rehash of Source MD5: BC39C3F7EE7A50E77B9BA1E65A5AEEF7
Results:	

Assertion & Expected Result	Actual Result
AM-01 Source acquired using interface AI.	as expected
AM-02 Source is type DS.	as expected
AM-03 Execution environment is XE.	as expected
AM-05 An image is created on file system type FS.	as expected
AM-06 All visible sectors acquired.	as expected
AM-08 All sectors accurately acquired.	as expected
AO-01 Image file is complete and accurate.	as expected
AO-05 Multifile image created.	as expected
AO-22 Tool calculates hashes by block.	option not available
AO-23 Logged information is correct.	as expected
AO-24 Source is unchanged by acquisition.	as expected

Analysis:	Expected results achieved

5.2.12   DA-07-F32

Test Case DA-07-F32 Linen 5.05f	
Case Summary:	DA-07 Acquire a digital source of type DS to an image file.
Assertions:	AM-01 The tool uses access interface SRC-AI to access the digital source. AM-02 The tool acquires digital source DS. AM-03 The tool executes in execution environment XE. AM-05 If image file creation is specified, the tool creates an image file on file system type FS. AM-06 All visible sectors are acquired from the digital source. AM-08 All sectors acquired from the digital source are acquired accurately. AO-01 If the tool creates an image file, the data represented by the image file is the same as the data acquired by the tool. AO-05 If the tool creates a multi-file image of a requested size then all the individual files shall be no larger than the requested size. AO-22 If requested, the tool calculates block hashes for a specified block size during an acquisition for each block acquired from the digital source. AO-23 If the tool logs any log significant information, the information is accurately recorded in the log file. AO-24 If the tool executes in a forensically safe execution environment, the digital source is unchanged by the acquisition process.
Tester Name:	brl
Test Host:	Max
Test Date:	Thu Feb 8 09:52:27 2007
Drives:	src(43) dst (none) other (EF)
Source Setup:	src hash (SHA1): < 888E2E7F7AD237DC7A732281DD93F325065E5871 > src hash (MD5): < BC39C3F7EE7A50E77B9BA1E65A5AEEF7 > 78125000 total sectors (40000000000 bytes) Model (0BB-75JHC0) serial # (WD-WMAMC46588) <pre>N Start LBA Length Start C/H/S End C/H/S boot Partition type
 1 P 000000063 020980827 0000/001/01 1023/254/63   0C Fat32X
 2 X 020980890 057143205 1023/000/01 1023/254/63   0F extended
 3 S 000000063 000032067 1023/001/01 1023/254/63   01 Fat12
 4 x 000032130 002104515 1023/000/01 1023/254/63   05 extended
 5 S 000000063 002104452 1023/001/01 1023/254/63   06 Fat16
 6 x 002136645 004192965 1023/000/01 1023/254/63   05 extended
 7 S 000000063 004192902 1023/001/01 1023/254/63   16 other
 8 x 006329610 008401995 1023/000/01 1023/254/63   05 extended
 9 S 000000063 008401932 1023/001/01 1023/254/63   0B Fat32
10 x 014731605 010490445 1023/000/01 1023/254/63   05 extended
11 S 000000063 010490382 1023/001/01 1023/254/63   83 Linux
12 x 025222050 004209030 1023/000/01 1023/254/63   05 extended
13 S 000000063 004208967 1023/001/01 1023/254/63   82 Linux swap
14 x 029431080 027712125 1023/000/01 1023/254/63   05 extended
15 S 000000063 027712062 1023/001/01 1023/254/63   07 NTFS
16 S 000000000 000000000 0000/000/00 0000/000/00   00 empty entry
17 P 000000000 000000000 0000/000/00 0000/000/00   00 empty entry
18 P 000000000 000000000 0000/000/00 0000/000/00   00 empty entry
 1 020980827 sectors 10742183424 bytes
 3 000032067 sectors 16418304 bytes
 5 002104452 sectors 1077479424 bytes
 7 004192902 sectors 2146765824 bytes
 9 008401932 sectors 4301789184 bytes
11 010490382 sectors 5371075584 bytes
13 004208967 sectors 2154991104 bytes
15 027712062 sectors 14188575744 bytes

Partition Hashes
43F12 md5sum 16418304 CBA0C9984F51778E89DEF0C6BED06864
43F16 md5sum 1077479424 37E81FFB31C3CB38AA48B2237500908E
43F32 md5sum 4301789184 2C4D8D450E5AD28329F616D87114CCFE
43F32x md5sum 10742183424 5980CB0FA68E9862C65765DF50F00906
43swap md5sum 2154991104 4B602964A30FE20D1B22B046A7375A7C
43x2 md5sum 5371075584 C7A84DE9ACBCB05463604CE8823D0874
43NTFS md5sum 14188575744 5D42FA317C802ACFEF2D313092D7411E</pre> |
| Log | Total Capacity:4,293,382,144 bytes (4GB) |

Test Case DA-07-F32 Linen 5.05f	
Highlights:	Total Clusters:1,048,189Unallocated:4,293,173,248 bytes (4GB) OEM Version:MSWIN4.1Serial Number:5559-6865 Actual Date:02/08/07 09:59:44AM File Integrity:Completely Verified, 0 Errors Acquisition Hash:2c4d8d450e5ad28329f616d87114ccfe Verify Hash:2c4d8d450e5ad28329f616d87114ccfe EnCase Version:5.05f System Version:Linux Error Granularity:64 Total Size:4,301,789,184 bytes (4GB) Total Sectors:8,401,932 Rehash of Source MD5: BC39C3F7EE7A50E77B9BA1E65A5AEEF7
Results:	

Assertion & Expected Result	Actual Result
AM-01 Source acquired using interface AI.	as expected
AM-02 Source is type DS.	as expected
AM-03 Execution environment is XE.	as expected
AM-05 An image is created on file system type FS.	as expected
AM-06 All visible sectors acquired.	as expected
AM-08 All sectors accurately acquired.	as expected
AO-01 Image file is complete and accurate.	as expected
AO-05 Multifile image created.	as expected
AO-22 Tool calculates hashes by block.	option not available
AO-23 Logged information is correct.	as expected
AO-24 Source is unchanged by acquisition.	as expected

Analysis:	Expected results achieved

5.2.13   DA-07-F32X

Test Case DA-07-F32X Linen 5.05f	
Case Summary:	DA-07 Acquire a digital source of type DS to an image file.
Assertions:	AM-01 The tool uses access interface SRC-AI to access the digital source. AM-02 The tool acquires digital source DS. AM-03 The tool executes in execution environment XE. AM-05 If image file creation is specified, the tool creates an image file on file system type FS. AM-06 All visible sectors are acquired from the digital source. AM-08 All sectors acquired from the digital source are acquired accurately. AO-01 If the tool creates an image file, the data represented by the image file is the same as the data acquired by the tool. AO-05 If the tool creates a multi-file image of a requested size then all the individual files shall be no larger than the requested size. AO-22 If requested, the tool calculates block hashes for a specified block size during an acquisition for each block acquired from the digital source. AO-23 If the tool logs any log significant information, the information is accurately recorded in the log file. AO-24 If the tool executes in a forensically safe execution environment, the digital source is unchanged by the acquisition process.
Tester Name:	brl
Test Host:	AndWife
Test Date:	Wed Feb 7 10:30:22 2007
Drives:	src(43) dst (none) other (52-IDE)
Source Setup:	src hash (SHA1): < 888E2E7F7AD237DC7A732281DD93F325065E5871 > src hash (MD5): < BC39C3F7EE7A50E77B9BA1E65A5AEEF7 > 78125000 total sectors (40000000000 bytes) Model (0BB-75JHC0) serial # (WD-WMAMC46588) N Start LBA Length Start C/H/S End C/H/S boot Partition type 1 P 000000063 020980827 0000/001/01 1023/254/63 0C Fat32X 2 X 020980890 057143205 1023/000/01 1023/254/63 0F extended 3 S 000000063 000032067 1023/001/01 1023/254/63 01 Fat12 4 x 000032130 002104515 1023/000/01 1023/254/63 05 extended 5 S 000000063 002104452 1023/001/01 1023/254/63 06 Fat16 6 x 002136645 004192965 1023/000/01 1023/254/63 05 extended 7 S 000000063 004192902 1023/001/01 1023/254/63 16 other 8 x 006329610 008401995 1023/000/01 1023/254/63 05 extended 9 S 000000063 008401932 1023/001/01 1023/254/63 0B Fat32 10 x 014731605 010490445 1023/000/01 1023/254/63 05 extended 11 S 000000063 010490382 1023/001/01 1023/254/63 83 Linux 12 x 025222050 004209030 1023/000/01 1023/254/63 05 extended 13 S 000000063 004208967 1023/001/01 1023/254/63 82 Linux swap 14 x 029431080 027712125 1023/000/01 1023/254/63 05 extended 15 S 000000063 027712062 1023/001/01 1023/254/63 07 NTFS 16 S 000000000 000000000 0000/000/00 0000/000/00 00 empty entry 17 P 000000000 000000000 0000/000/00 0000/000/00 00 empty entry 18 P 000000000 000000000 0000/000/00 0000/000/00 00 empty entry 1 020980827 sectors 10742183424 bytes 3 000032067 sectors 16418304 bytes 5 002104452 sectors 1077479424 bytes 7 004192902 sectors 2146765824 bytes 9 008401932 sectors 4301789184 bytes 11 010490382 sectors 5371075584 bytes 13 004208967 sectors 2154991104 bytes 15 027712062 sectors 14188575744 bytes Partition Hashes 43F12 md5sum 16418304 CBA0C9984F51778E89DEF0C6BED06864 43F16 md5sum 1077479424 37E81FFB31C3CB38AA48B2237500908E 43F32 md5sum 4301789184 2C4D8D450E5AD28329F616D87114CCFE 43F32x md5sum 10742183424 5980CB0FA68E9862C65765DF50F00906 43swap md5sum 2154991104 4B602964A30FE20D1B22B046A7375A7C 43x2 md5sum 5371075584 C7A84DE9ACBCB05463604CE8823D0874 43NTFS md5sum 14188575744 5D42FA317C802ACFEF2D313092D7411E
Log	Total Capacity:10,731,683,840 bytes (10GB)

Test Case DA-07-F32X Linen 5.05f

Highlights:	Total Clusters:1,310,020Unallocated:10,729,906,176 bytes (10GB) OEM Version:MSWIN4.1Serial Number:4445-13C7 Actual Date:02/07/07 10:35:56AM File Integrity:Completely Verified, 0 Errors Acquisition Hash:5980cb0fa68e9862c65765df50f00906 Verify Hash:5980cb0fa68e9862c65765df50f00906 EnCase Version:5.05f System Version:Linux Error Granularity:64 Total Size:10,742,183,424 bytes (10GB) Total Sectors:20,980,827 Rehash of Source MD5: BC39C3F7EE7A50E77B9BA1E65A5AEEF7

Results:

Assertion & Expected Result	Actual Result
AM-01 Source acquired using interface AI.	as expected
AM-02 Source is type DS.	as expected
AM-03 Execution environment is XE.	as expected
AM-05 An image is created on file system type FS.	as expected
AM-06 All visible sectors acquired.	as expected
AM-08 All sectors accurately acquired.	as expected
AO-01 Image file is complete and accurate.	as expected
AO-05 Multifile image created.	as expected
AO-22 Tool calculates hashes by block.	option not available
AO-23 Logged information is correct.	as expected
AO-24 Source is unchanged by acquisition.	as expected

Analysis:	Expected results achieved

5.2.14 DA-07-THUMB

Test Case DA-07-THUMB Linen 5.05f	
Case Summary:	DA-07 Acquire a digital source of type DS to an image file.
Assertions:	AM-01 The tool uses access interface SRC-AI to access the digital source.
	AM-02 The tool acquires digital source DS.
	AM-03 The tool executes in execution environment XE.
	AM-05 If image file creation is specified, the tool creates an image file on file system type FS.
	AM-06 All visible sectors are acquired from the digital source.
	AM-08 All sectors acquired from the digital source are acquired accurately.
	AO-01 If the tool creates an image file, the data represented by the image file is the same as the data acquired by the tool.
	AO-05 If the tool creates a multi-file image of a requested size then all the individual files shall be no larger than the requested size.
	AO-22 If requested, the tool calculates block hashes for a specified block size during an acquisition for each block acquired from the digital source.
	AO-23 If the tool logs any log significant information, the information is accurately recorded in the log file.
	AO-24 If the tool executes in a forensically safe execution environment, the digital source is unchanged by the acquisition process.
Tester Name:	brl
Test Host:	Max
Test Date:	Thu Feb 8 11:54:55 2007
Drives:	src(D5-THUMB) dst (none) other (EF)
Source Setup:	src hash (SHA1): < D68520EF74A336E49DCCF83815B7B08FDC53E38A >
	src hash (MD5): < C843593624B2B3B878596D8760B19954 >
	505856 total sectors (258998272 bytes)
	Model (usb2.0Flash Disk) serial # ()
	N Start LBA Length Start C/H/S End C/H/S boot Partition type
	1 P 778135908 1141509631 0357/116/40 0357/032/45 Boot 72 other
	2 P 168689522 1936028240 0288/115/43 0367/114/50 Boot 65 other
	3 P 1869881465 1936028192 0366/032/33 0357/032/43 Boot 79 other
	4 P 2885681152 000055499 0372/097/50 0000/010/00 Boot 0D other
	1 1141509631 sectors 584452931072 bytes
	2 1936028240 sectors 991246458880 bytes
	3 1936028192 sectors 991246434304 bytes
	4 000055499 sectors 28415488 bytes
Log Highlights:	Actual Date:02/08/07 11:59:09AM
	File Integrity:Completely Verified, 0 Errors
	Acquisition Hash:c843593624b2b3b878596d8760b19954
	Verify Hash:c843593624b2b3b878596d8760b19954
	EnCase Version:5.05f
	System Version:Linux
	Error Granularity:64
	Total Size:258,998,272 bytes (247MB)
	Total Sectors:505,856
	Rehash of Source MD5: C843593624B2B3B878596D8760B19954

Results:		
	Assertion & Expected Result	**Actual Result**
	AM-01 Source acquired using interface AI.	as expected
	AM-02 Source is type DS.	as expected
	AM-03 Execution environment is XE.	as expected
	AM-05 An image is created on file system type FS.	as expected
	AM-06 All visible sectors acquired.	as expected
	AM-08 All sectors accurately acquired.	as expected
	AO-01 Image file is complete and accurate.	as expected
	AO-05 Multifile image created.	as expected
	AO-22 Tool calculates hashes by block.	option not available
	AO-23 Logged information is correct.	as expected
	AO-24 Source is unchanged by acquisition.	as expected

Test Case DA-07-THUMB Linen 5.05f	
Analysis:	Expected results achieved

5.2.15   DA-07-X2

Test Case DA-07-X2 Linen 5.05f	
Case Summary:	DA-07 Acquire a digital source of type DS to an image file.
Assertions:	AM-01 The tool uses access interface SRC-AI to access the digital source. AM-02 The tool acquires digital source DS. AM-03 The tool executes in execution environment XE. AM-05 If image file creation is specified, the tool creates an image file on file system type FS. AM-06 All visible sectors are acquired from the digital source. AM-08 All sectors acquired from the digital source are acquired accurately. AO-01 If the tool creates an image file, the data represented by the image file is the same as the data acquired by the tool. AO-05 If the tool creates a multi-file image of a requested size then all the individual files shall be no larger than the requested size. AO-22 If requested, the tool calculates block hashes for a specified block size during an acquisition for each block acquired from the digital source. AO-23 If the tool logs any log significant information, the information is accurately recorded in the log file. AO-24 If the tool executes in a forensically safe execution environment, the digital source is unchanged by the acquisition process.
Tester Name:	brl
Test Host:	Max
Test Date:	Thu Feb 8 16:15:59 2007
Drives:	src(43) dst (none) other (EF)

Source Setup:	src hash (SHA1): < 888E2E7F7AD237DC7A732281DD93F325065E5871 >
	src hash (MD5): < BC39C3F7EE7A50E77B9BA1E65A5AEEF7 >
	78125000 total sectors (40000000000 bytes)
	Model (0BB-75JHC0) serial # (WD-WMAMC46588)
	<pre>N Start LBA Length Start C/H/S End C/H/S boot Partition type
	 1 P 000000063 020980827 0000/001/01 1023/254/63 0C Fat32X
	 2 X 020980890 057143205 1023/000/01 1023/254/63 0F extended
	 3 S 000000063 000032067 1023/001/01 1023/254/63 01 Fat12
	 4 x 000032130 002104515 1023/000/01 1023/254/63 05 extended
	 5 S 000000063 002104452 1023/001/01 1023/254/63 06 Fat16
	 6 x 002136645 004192965 1023/000/01 1023/254/63 05 extended
	 7 S 000000063 004192902 1023/001/01 1023/254/63 16 other
	 8 x 006329610 008401995 1023/000/01 1023/254/63 05 extended
	 9 S 000000063 008401932 1023/001/01 1023/254/63 0B Fat32
	10 x 014731605 010490445 1023/000/01 1023/254/63 05 extended
	11 S 000000063 010490382 1023/001/01 1023/254/63 83 Linux
	12 x 025222050 004209030 1023/000/01 1023/254/63 05 extended
	13 S 000000063 004208967 1023/001/01 1023/254/63 82 Linux swap
	14 x 029431080 027712125 1023/000/01 1023/254/63 05 extended
	15 S 000000063 027712062 1023/001/01 1023/254/63 07 NTFS
	16 S 000000000 000000000 0000/000/00 0000/000/00 00 empty entry
	17 P 000000000 000000000 0000/000/00 0000/000/00 00 empty entry
	18 P 000000000 000000000 0000/000/00 0000/000/00 00 empty entry
	 1 020980827 sectors 10742183424 bytes
	 3 000032067 sectors 16418304 bytes
	 5 002104452 sectors 1077479424 bytes
	 7 004192902 sectors 2146765824 bytes
	 9 008401932 sectors 4301789184 bytes
	11 010490382 sectors 5371075584 bytes
	13 004208967 sectors 2154991104 bytes
	15 027712062 sectors 14188575744 bytes
	
	Partition Hashes
	43F12 md5sum 16418304 CBA0C9984F51778E89DEF0C6BED06864
	43F16 md5sum 1077479424 37E81FFB31C3CB38AA48B2237500908E
	43F32 md5sum 4301789184 2C4D8D450E5AD28329F616D87114CCFE
	43F32x md5sum 10742183424 5980CB0FA68E9862C65765DF50F00906
	43swap md5sum 2154991104 4B602964A30FE20D1B22B046A7375A7C
	43x2 md5sum 5371075584 C7A84DE9ACBCB05463604CE8823D0874
	43NTFS md5sum 14188575744 5D42FA317C802ACFEF2D313092D7411E</pre>

Log	Total Capacity:5,371,075,584 bytes (5GB)

Test Case DA-07-X2 Linen 5.05f	
Highlights:	Total Clusters:5,245,191Unallocated:5,187,181,568 bytes (4.8GB) Actual Date:02/08/07 04:19:53PM File Integrity:Completely Verified, 0 Errors Acquisition Hash:c7a84de9acbcb05463604ce8823d0874 Verify Hash:c7a84de9acbcb05463604ce8823d0874 EnCase Version:5.05f System Version:Linux Error Granularity:64 Total Size:5,371,075,584 bytes (5GB) Total Sectors:10,490,382 Rehash of Source MD5: BC39C3F7EE7A50E77B9BA1E65A5AEEF7
Results:	

Assertion & Expected Result	Actual Result
AM-01 Source acquired using interface AI.	as expected
AM-02 Source is type DS.	as expected
AM-03 Execution environment is XE.	as expected
AM-05 An image is created on file system type FS.	as expected
AM-06 All visible sectors acquired.	as expected
AM-08 All sectors accurately acquired.	as expected
AO-01 Image file is complete and accurate.	as expected
AO-05 Multifile image created.	as expected
AO-22 Tool calculates hashes by block.	option not available
AO-23 Logged information is correct.	as expected
AO-24 Source is unchanged by acquisition.	as expected

Analysis:	Expected results achieved

5.2.16   DA-08-ATA28

Test Case DA-08-ATA28 Linen 5.05f	
Case Summary:	DA-08 Acquire a physical drive with hidden sectors to an image file.
Assertions:	AM-01 The tool uses access interface SRC-AI to access the digital source. AM-02 The tool acquires digital source DS. AM-03 The tool executes in execution environment XE. AM-05 If image file creation is specified, the tool creates an image file on file system type FS. AM-06 All visible sectors are acquired from the digital source. AM-07 All hidden sectors are acquired from the digital source. AM-08 All sectors acquired from the digital source are acquired accurately. AO-01 If the tool creates an image file, the data represented by the image file is the same as the data acquired by the tool. AO-05 If the tool creates a multi-file image of a requested size then all the individual files shall be no larger than the requested size. AO-22 If requested, the tool calculates block hashes for a specified block size during an acquisition for each block acquired from the digital source. AO-23 If the tool logs any log significant information, the information is accurately recorded in the log file. AO-24 If the tool executes in a forensically safe execution environment, the digital source is unchanged by the acquisition process.
Tester Name:	brl
Test Host:	AndWife
Test Date:	Mon Feb 5 13:20:03 2007
Drives:	src(42) dst (none) other (28-IDE)
Source Setup:	src hash (SHA1): < 5A75399023056E0EB905082B35F8FAA1DB049229 > src hash (MD5): < F4B9AAB24554EEEB2A962BDA554A9252 > 78165360 total sectors (40020664320 bytes) 65534/015/63 (max cyl/hd values) 65535/016/63 (number of cyl/hd) IDE disk: Model (WDC WD400JB-00JJC0) serial # (WD-WCAMA3958512) N Start LBA Length Start C/H/S End C/H/S boot Partition type 1 P 000000063 070348572 0000/001/01 1023/254/63 Boot 07 NTFS 2 P 000000000 000000000 0000/000/00 0000/000/00 00 empty entry 3 P 000000000 000000000 0000/000/00 0000/000/00 00 empty entry 4 P 000000000 000000000 0000/000/00 0000/000/00 00 empty entry 1 070348572 sectors 36018468864 bytes HPA created BIOS, XBIOS and Direct disk geometry Reporter (BXDR) BXDR 128 /S70000000 /P /fbxdrlog.txt Setting Maximum Addressable Sector to 70000000 MAS now set to 70000000 Hashes with HPA in place md5:9BF3C3DEADE47056A1DDC073C5F6B2E2 sha1:D76F909482B00767B62C295CADE202F92E61CD2E
Log Highlights:	Actual Date:02/05/07 01:26:02PM File Integrity:Completely Verified, 0 Errors Acquisition Hash:f4b9aab24554eeeb2a962bda554a9252 Verify Hash:f4b9aab24554eeeb2a962bda554a9252 EnCase Version:5.05f System Version:Linux Error Granularity:64 Total Size:40,020,664,320 bytes (37.3GB) Total Sectors:78,165,360 Rehash of Source MD5: 9BF3C3DEADE47056A1DDC073C5F6B2E2
Results:	

Assertion & Expected Result	Actual Result
AM-01 Source acquired using interface AI.	as expected
AM-02 Source is type DS.	as expected
AM-03 Execution environment is XE.	as expected
AM-05 An image is created on file system type FS.	as expected

Test Case DA-08-ATA28 Linen 5.05f		
	AM-06 All visible sectors acquired.	as expected
	AM-07 All hidden sectors acquired.	as expected
	AM-08 All sectors accurately acquired.	as expected
	AO-01 Image file is complete and accurate.	as expected
	AO-05 Multifile image created.	as expected
	AO-22 Tool calculates hashes by block.	option not available
	AO-23 Logged information is correct.	as expected
	AO-24 Source is unchanged by acquisition.	as expected
Analysis:	Expected results achieved	

5.2.17   DA-08-ATA48

Test Case DA-08-ATA48 Linen 5.05f	
Case Summary:	DA-08 Acquire a physical drive with hidden sectors to an image file.
Assertions:	AM-01 The tool uses access interface SRC-AI to access the digital source. AM-02 The tool acquires digital source DS. AM-03 The tool executes in execution environment XE. AM-05 If image file creation is specified, the tool creates an image file on file system type FS. AM-06 All visible sectors are acquired from the digital source. AM-07 All hidden sectors are acquired from the digital source. AM-08 All sectors acquired from the digital source are acquired accurately. AO-01 If the tool creates an image file, the data represented by the image file is the same as the data acquired by the tool. AO-05 If the tool creates a multi-file image of a requested size then all the individual files shall be no larger than the requested size. AO-22 If requested, the tool calculates block hashes for a specified block size during an acquisition for each block acquired from the digital source. AO-23 If the tool logs any log significant information, the information is accurately recorded in the log file. AO-24 If the tool executes in a forensically safe execution environment, the digital source is unchanged by the acquisition process.
Tester Name:	brl
Test Host:	Joe
Test Date:	Tue Feb 6 17:32:06 2007
Drives:	src(4B) dst (none) other (28-IDE)
Source Setup:	src hash (SHA1): < F409920836FED76DBB60DEEEF467A6DDED5BF48E > src hash (MD5): < B5641B5A594912B4D60518304B1DE698 > 390721968 total sectors (200049647616 bytes) 24320/254/63 (max cyl/hd values) 24321/255/63 (number of cyl/hd) IDE disk: Model (WDC WD2000JB-00GVC0) serial # (WD-WCAL78252964) N Start LBA Length Start C/H/S End C/H/S boot Partition type 1 P 000000063 351646722 0000/001/01 1023/254/63 Boot 07 NTFS 2 P 000000000 000000000 0000/000/00 0000/000/00 00 empty entry 3 P 000000000 000000000 0000/000/00 0000/000/00 00 empty entry 4 P 000000000 000000000 0000/000/00 0000/000/00 00 empty entry 1 351646722 sectors 180043121664 bytes HPA created BIOS, XBIOS and Direct disk geometry Reporter (BXDR) BXDR 128 /S351000000 /P /fHPA.TXT Setting Maximum Addressable Sector to 351000000 MAS now set to 351000000 Hashes with HPA in place md5:6BAFEFC000470C126434D933429C879B sha1:2D50DBD82CD3DA90A6E5BF13B2B40808C40998A1
Log Highlights:	Actual Date:02/06/07 05:33:25PM File Integrity:Completely Verified, 0 Errors Acquisition Hash:b5641b5a594912b4d60518304b1de698 Verify Hash:b5641b5a594912b4d60518304b1de698 EnCase Version:5.05f System Version:Linux Error Granularity:64 Total Size:200,049,647,616 bytes (186.3GB) Total Sectors:390,721,968 Rehash of Source MD5: 6BAFEFC000470C126434D933429C879B
Results:	

Assertion & Expected Result	Actual Result
AM-01 Source acquired using interface AI.	as expected
AM-02 Source is type DS.	as expected
AM-03 Execution environment is XE.	as expected
AM-05 An image is created on file system type FS.	as expected

Test Case DA-08-ATA48 Linen 5.05f		
	AM-06 All visible sectors acquired.	as expected
	AM-07 All hidden sectors acquired.	as expected
	AM-08 All sectors accurately acquired.	as expected
	AO-01 Image file is complete and accurate.	as expected
	AO-05 Multifile image created.	as expected
	AO-22 Tool calculates hashes by block.	option not available
	AO-23 Logged information is correct.	as expected
	AO-24 Source is unchanged by acquisition.	as expected
Analysis:	Expected results achieved	

5.2.18   DA-08-DCO

Test Case DA-08-DCO Linen 5.05f	
Case Summary:	DA-08 Acquire a physical drive with hidden sectors to an image file.
Assertions:	AM-01 The tool uses access interface SRC-AI to access the digital source. AM-02 The tool acquires digital source DS. AM-03 The tool executes in execution environment XE. AM-05 If image file creation is specified, the tool creates an image file on file system type FS. AM-06 All visible sectors are acquired from the digital source. AM-07 All hidden sectors are acquired from the digital source. AM-08 All sectors acquired from the digital source are acquired accurately. AO-01 If the tool creates an image file, the data represented by the image file is the same as the data acquired by the tool. AO-05 If the tool creates a multi-file image of a requested size then all the individual files shall be no larger than the requested size. AO-22 If requested, the tool calculates block hashes for a specified block size during an acquisition for each block acquired from the digital source. AO-23 If the tool logs any log significant information, the information is accurately recorded in the log file. AO-24 If the tool executes in a forensically safe execution environment, the digital source is unchanged by the acquisition process.
Tester Name:	brl
Test Host:	Max
Test Date:	Fri Jan 19 11:15:45 2007
Drives:	src(92) dst (none) other (EF)
Source Setup:	src hash (SHA1): < 63E6F7BD3040A8ADA2CF8FBF66A805B76DF10481 > src hash (MD5): < E095DD1BD0B0DD6E603153A3FE1A2F3E > 58633344 total sectors (30020272128 bytes) 58167/015/63 (max cyl/hd values) 58168/016/63 (number of cyl/hd) IDE disk: Model (WDC WD300BB-00CAA0) serial # (WD-WMA8H2140350) N Start LBA Length Start C/H/S End C/H/S boot Partition type 1 P 000000063 058605057 0000/001/01 1023/254/63 Boot 07 NTFS 2 P 000000000 000000000 0000/000/00 0000/000/00 00 empty entry 3 P 000000000 000000000 0000/000/00 0000/000/00 00 empty entry 4 P 000000000 000000000 0000/000/00 0000/000/00 00 empty entry 1 058605057 sectors 30005789184 bytes Hashes with DCO in place: md5:525963C6789423396FE1F3202A8CBD04 sha1.txt:55A3CFE756B7B0034DCCE71F7D7A477D8681B781
Log Highlights:	Actual Date:01/19/07 11:36:17AM File Integrity:Completely Verified, 0 Errors Acquisition Hash:525963c6789423396fe1f3202a8cbd04 Verify Hash:525963c6789423396fe1f3202a8cbd04 EnCase Version:5.05f System Version:Linux Error Granularity:64 Total Size:27,018,245,120 bytes (25.2GB) Total Sectors:52,770,010 Rehash of Source MD5: 525963C6789423396FE1F3202A8CBD04
Results:	

Assertion & Expected Result	Actual Result
AM-01 Source acquired using interface AI.	as expected
AM-02 Source is type DS.	as expected
AM-03 Execution environment is XE.	as expected
AM-05 An image is created on file system type FS.	as expected
AM-06 All visible sectors acquired.	as expected
AM-07 All hidden sectors acquired.	DCO not acquired
AM-08 All sectors accurately acquired.	as expected
AO-01 Image file is complete and accurate.	as expected

Test Case DA-08-DCO Linen 5.05f		
	AO-22 Tool calculates hashes by block.	option not available
	AO-23 Logged information is correct.	as expected
	AO-24 Source is unchanged by acquisition.	as expected
Analysis:	Expected results not achieved	

5.2.19   DA-09-01

Test Case DA-09-01 Linen 5.05f	
Case Summary:	DA-09 Acquire a digital source that has at least one faulty data sector.
Assertions:	AM-01 The tool uses access interface SRC-AI to access the digital source. AM-02 The tool acquires digital source DS. AM-03 The tool executes in execution environment XE. AM-05 If image file creation is specified, the tool creates an image file on file system type FS. AM-06 All visible sectors are acquired from the digital source. AM-08 All sectors acquired from the digital source are acquired accurately. AM-09 If unresolved errors occur while reading from the selected digital source, the tool notifies the user of the error type and location within the digital source. AM-10 If unresolved errors occur while reading from the selected digital source, the tool uses a benign fill in the destination object in place of the inaccessible data. AO-01 If the tool creates an image file, the data represented by the image file is the same as the data acquired by the tool. AO-05 If the tool creates a multi-file image of a requested size then all the individual files shall be no larger than the requested size. AO-22 If requested, the tool calculates block hashes for a specified block size during an acquisition for each block acquired from the digital source. AO-23 If the tool logs any log significant information, the information is accurately recorded in the log file. AO-24 If the tool executes in a forensically safe execution environment, the digital source is unchanged by the acquisition process.
Tester Name:	brl
Test Host:	Max
Test Date:	Mon Feb 5 10:35:47 2007
Drives:	src(ED-BAD-CPR1) dst (F3) other (EF)
Source Setup:	No before hash for ED-BAD-CPR1 120103200 total sectors (61492838400 bytes) Drive with known bad sectors Vendor: Maxtor Model: DiamondMax Plus 9 Known Bad Sector List for ED-CPR-BAD-1 Manufacturer: Maxtor Model: 6Y060L0 DiamondMax Plus 9 Serial Number: Y27KR6CE Capacity: 60GB Interface: PATA 10069095, 10069911, 12023808, 18652594, 18656041, 18656857, 18660303, 18661119, 19746716-19746717, 22233904, 23098370, 23383001, 24102466-24102467, 24104250, 24106656, 24107458, 28959971-28959972, 41825791, 41828995, 52654580, 52655318, 60522984, 68643842-68643843, 69973290, 72714626, 72715293, 82148809, 82148810, 83810525, 85310861, 85313430, 85314038-85314039, 86321211, 86323780, 87186066, 87856313, 87856922, 97191260-97191261, 100093150-100093151, 103861021, 109706975-109706976, 110347947, 110350122-110350123, 115664758, 115835518
Log Highlights:	Destination setup 156301488 sectors wiped with F3 Comparision of original to clone Drive Sectors compared: 120103200 Sectors match: 120102840 Sectors differ: 360 Bytes differ: 183960 Diffs range 10069088-10069095, 10069904-10069911, 12023808-12023815, 18652592-18652599, 18656040-18656047, 18656856-18656863, 18660296-18660303, 18661112-18661119, 19746712-19746719, 22233904-22233911, 23098368-23098375, 23383000-23383007, 24102464-24102471, 24104248-24104255, 24106656-24106663, 24107456-24107463, 28959968-28959975, 41825784-41825791,

```
41828992-41828999, 52654576-52654583, 52655312-52655319,
60522984-60522991, 68643840-68643847, 69973288-69973295,
72714624-72714631, 72715288-72715295, 82148808-82148815,
83810520-83810527, 85310856-85310863, 85313424-85313431,
85314032-85314039, 86321208-86321215, 86323776-86323783,
87186064-87186071, 87856312-87856319, 87856920-87856927,
97191256-97191263, 100093144-100093151, 103861016-103861023,
109706968-109706983, 110347944-110347951, 110350120-110350127,
115664752-115664759, 115835512-115835519
Source (120103200) has 36198288 fewer sectors than destination (156301488)
Zero fill:                     0
Src Byte fill (ED):            0
Dst Byte fill (F0):            0
Other fill (F3):     36198288
Other no fill:                 0
Zero fill range:
Src fill range:
Dst fill range:
Other fill range:   120103200-156301487
Other not filled range:
0 source read errors, 0 destination read errors

Actual Date:02/05/07 10:44:30AM
File Integrity:Completely Verified, 0 Errors
Acquisition Hash:e31c68c558503ecd0b7781bb5c942fbb
Verify Hash:e31c68c558503ecd0b7781bb5c942fbb
EnCase Version:5.05f
System Version:Linux
Error Granularity:1
Read Errors:44
Total Size:61,492,838,400 bytes (57.3GB)
Total Sectors:120,103,200
Read errors:
  10,069,088  (8)
  10,069,904  (8)
  12,023,808  (8)
  18,652,592  (8)
  18,656,040  (8)
  18,656,856  (8)
  18,660,296  (8)
  18,661,112  (8)
  19,746,712  (8)
  22,233,904  (8)
  23,098,368  (8)
  23,383,000  (8)
  24,102,464  (8)
  24,104,248  (8)
  24,106,656  (8)
  24,107,456  (8)
  28,959,968  (8)
  41,825,784  (8)
  41,828,992  (8)
  52,654,576  (8)
  52,655,312  (8)
  60,522,984  (8)
  68,643,840  (8)
  69,973,288  (8)
  72,714,624  (8)
  72,715,288  (8)
  82,148,808  (8)
  83,810,520  (8)
  85,310,856  (8)
  85,313,424  (8)
  85,314,032  (8)
  86,321,208  (8)
  86,323,776  (8)
  87,186,064  (8)
  87,856,312  (8)
  87,856,920  (8)
  97,191,256  (8)
```

Test Case DA-09-01 Linen 5.05f

```
100,093,144  (8)
103,861,016  (8)
109,706,968  (16)
110,347,944  (8)
110,350,120  (8)
115,664,752  (8)
115,835,512  (8)
```

Results:

Assertion & Expected Result	Actual Result
AM-01 Source acquired using interface AI.	as expected
AM-02 Source is type DS.	as expected
AM-03 Execution environment is XE.	as expected
AM-05 An image is created on file system type FS.	as expected
AM-06 All visible sectors acquired.	as expected
AM-08 All sectors accurately acquired.	some sectors differ
AM-09 Error logged.	as expected
AM-10 Benign fill replaces inaccessible sectors.	as expected
AO-01 Image file is complete and accurate.	as expected
AO-05 Multifile image created.	as expected
AO-22 Tool calculates hashes by block.	option not available
AO-23 Logged information is correct.	as expected
AO-24 Source is unchanged by acquisition.	as expected

Analysis: | Expected results not achieved

5.2.20   DA-09-02

Test Case DA-09-02 Linen 5.05f	
Case Summary:	DA-09 Acquire a digital source that has at least one faulty data sector.
Assertions:	AM-01 The tool uses access interface SRC-AI to access the digital source. AM-02 The tool acquires digital source DS. AM-03 The tool executes in execution environment XE. AM-05 If image file creation is specified, the tool creates an image file on file system type FS. AM-06 All visible sectors are acquired from the digital source. AM-08 All sectors acquired from the digital source are acquired accurately. AM-09 If unresolved errors occur while reading from the selected digital source, the tool notifies the user of the error type and location within the digital source. AM-10 If unresolved errors occur while reading from the selected digital source, the tool uses a benign fill in the destination object in place of the inaccessible data. AO-01 If the tool creates an image file, the data represented by the image file is the same as the data acquired by the tool. AO-05 If the tool creates a multi-file image of a requested size then all the individual files shall be no larger than the requested size. AO-22 If requested, the tool calculates block hashes for a specified block size during an acquisition for each block acquired from the digital source. AO-23 If the tool logs any log significant information, the information is accurately recorded in the log file. AO-24 If the tool executes in a forensically safe execution environment, the digital source is unchanged by the acquisition process.
Tester Name:	brl
Test Host:	AndWife
Test Date:	Mon Jan 22 09:46:16 2007
Drives:	src(ED-BAD-CPR1) dst (06) other (EF)
Source Setup:	No before hash for ED-BAD-CPR1 120103200 total sectors (61492838400 bytes) Drive with known bad sectors Vendor: Maxtor Model: DiamondMax Plus 9 Known Bad Sector List for ED-CPR-BAD-1 Manufacturer: Maxtor Model: 6Y060L0 DiamondMax Plus 9 Serial Number: Y27KR6CE Capacity: 60GB Interface: PATA 10069095, 10069911, 12023808, 18652594, 18656041, 18656857, 18660303, 18661119, 19746716-19746717, 22233904, 23098370, 23383001, 24102466-24102467, 24104250, 24106656, 24107458, 28959971-28959972, 41825791, 41828995, 52654580, 52655318, 60522984, 68643842-68643843, 69973290, 72714626, 72715293, 82148809, 82148810, 83810525, 85310861, 85313430, 85314038-85314039, 86321211, 86323780, 87186066, 87856313, 87856922, 97191260-97191261, 100093150-100093151, 103861021, 109706975-109706976, 110347947, 110350122-110350123, 115664758, 115835518
Log Highlights:	Destination setup 156301488 sectors wiped with 6 Comparision of original to clone Drive Sectors compared: 120103200 Sectors match: 120102840 Sectors differ: 360 Bytes differ: 183960 Diffs range 10069088-10069095, 10069904-10069911, 12023808-12023815, 18652592-18652599, 18656040-18656047, 18656856-18656863, 18660296-18660303, 18661112-18661119, 19746712-19746719, 22233904-22233911, 23098368-23098375, 23383000-23383007, 24102464-24102471, 24104248-24104255, 24106656-24106663, 24107456-24107463, 28959968-28959975, 41825784-41825791,

```
41828992-41828999, 52654576-52654583, 52655312-52655319,
60522984-60522991, 68643840-68643847, 69973288-69973295,
72714624-72714631, 72715288-72715295, 82148808-82148815,
83810520-83810527, 85310856-85310863, 85313424-85313431,
85314032-85314039, 86321208-86321215, 86323776-86323783,
87186064-87186071, 87856312-87856319, 87856920-87856927,
97191256-97191263, 100093144-100093151, 103861016-103861023,
109706968-109706983, 110347944-110347951, 110350120-110350127,
115664752-115664759, 115835512-115835519
Source (120103200) has 36198288 fewer sectors than destination (156301488)
Zero fill:                      0
Src Byte fill (ED):             0
Dst Byte fill (06): 36198288
Other fill:                     0
Other no fill:                  0
Zero fill range:
Src fill range:
Dst fill range:   120103200-156301487
Other fill range:
Other not filled range:
0 source read errors, 0 destination read errors

Actual Date:01/22/07 09:48:36AM
File Integrity:Completely Verified, 0 Errors
Acquisition Hash:e31c68c558503ecd0b7781bb5c942fbb
Verify Hash:e31c68c558503ecd0b7781bb5c942fbb
EnCase Version:5.05f
System Version:Linux
Error Granularity:2
Read Errors:44
Total Size:61,492,838,400 bytes (57.3GB)
Total Sectors:120,103,200
Read errors:
  10,069,088  (8)
  10,069,904  (8)
  12,023,808  (8)
  18,652,592  (8)
  18,656,040  (8)
  18,656,856  (8)
  18,660,296  (8)
  18,661,112  (8)
  19,746,712  (8)
  22,233,904  (8)
  23,098,368  (8)
  23,383,000  (8)
  24,102,464  (8)
  24,104,248  (8)
  24,106,656  (8)
  24,107,456  (8)
  28,959,968  (8)
  41,825,784  (8)
  41,828,992  (8)
  52,654,576  (8)
  52,655,312  (8)
  60,522,984  (8)
  68,643,840  (8)
  69,973,288  (8)
  72,714,624  (8)
  72,715,288  (8)
  82,148,808  (8)
  83,810,520  (8)
  85,310,856  (8)
  85,313,424  (8)
  85,314,032  (8)
  86,321,208  (8)
  86,323,776  (8)
  87,186,064  (8)
  87,856,312  (8)
  87,856,920  (8)
  97,191,256  (8)
```

Test Case DA-09-02 Linen 5.05f	
	100,093,144 (8)
	103,861,016 (8)
	109,706,968 (16)
	110,347,944 (8)
	110,350,120 (8)
	115,664,752 (8)
	115,835,512 (8)

Results:		
	Assertion & Expected Result	**Actual Result**
	AM-01 Source acquired using interface AI.	as expected
	AM-02 Source is type DS.	as expected
	AM-03 Execution environment is XE.	as expected
	AM-05 An image is created on file system type FS.	as expected
	AM-06 All visible sectors acquired.	as expected
	AM-08 All sectors accurately acquired.	some sectors differ
	AM-09 Error logged.	as expected
	AM-10 Benign fill replaces inaccessible sectors.	as expected
	AO-01 Image file is complete and accurate.	as expected
	AO-05 Multifile image created.	as expected
	AO-22 Tool calculates hashes by block.	option not available
	AO-23 Logged information is correct.	as expected
	AO-24 Source is unchanged by acquisition.	as expected

Analysis:	Expected results not achieved

5.2.21   DA-09-16

Test Case DA-09-16 Linen 5.05f	
Case Summary:	DA-09 Acquire a digital source that has at least one faulty data sector.
Assertions:	AM-01 The tool uses access interface SRC-AI to access the digital source. AM-02 The tool acquires digital source DS. AM-03 The tool executes in execution environment XE. AM-05 If image file creation is specified, the tool creates an image file on file system type FS. AM-06 All visible sectors are acquired from the digital source. AM-08 All sectors acquired from the digital source are acquired accurately. AM-09 If unresolved errors occur while reading from the selected digital source, the tool notifies the user of the error type and location within the digital source. AM-10 If unresolved errors occur while reading from the selected digital source, the tool uses a benign fill in the destination object in place of the inaccessible data. AO-01 If the tool creates an image file, the data represented by the image file is the same as the data acquired by the tool. AO-05 If the tool creates a multi-file image of a requested size then all the individual files shall be no larger than the requested size. AO-22 If requested, the tool calculates block hashes for a specified block size during an acquisition for each block acquired from the digital source. AO-23 If the tool logs any log significant information, the information is accurately recorded in the log file. AO-24 If the tool executes in a forensically safe execution environment, the digital source is unchanged by the acquisition process.
Tester Name:	brl
Test Host:	Paladin
Test Date:	Tue Jan 23 15:38:52 2007
Drives:	src(ED-BAD-CPR1) dst (F3) other (EF)

Source Setup:	No before hash for ED-BAD-CPR1 120103200 total sectors (61492838400 bytes)
	  Drive with known bad sectors
	  Vendor: Maxtor Model: DiamondMax Plus 9
	
	Known Bad Sector List for ED-CPR-BAD-1
	
	Manufacturer: Maxtor
	Model: 6Y060L0 DiamondMax Plus 9
	Serial Number: Y27KR6CE
	Capacity: 60GB
	Interface: PATA
	
	10069095, 10069911, 12023808, 18652594, 18656041, 18656857, 18660303, 18661119, 19746716-19746717, 22233904, 23098370, 23383001, 24102466-24102467, 24104250, 24106656, 24107458, 28959971-28959972, 41825791, 41828995, 52654580, 52655318, 60522984, 68643842-68643843, 69973290, 72714626, 72715293, 82148809, 82148810, 83810525, 85310861, 85313430, 85314038-85314039, 86321211, 86323780, 87186066, 87856313, 87856922, 97191260-97191261, 100093150-100093151, 103861021, 109706975-109706976, 110347947, 110350122-110350123, 115664758, 115835518

Log Highlights:	Destination setup 156301488 sectors wiped with F3 Comparision of original to clone Drive Sectors compared: 120103200 Sectors match: 120102480 Sectors differ: 720 Bytes differ: 367920 Diffs range 10069088-10069103, 10069904-10069919, 12023808-12023823, 18652592-18652607, 18656032-18656047, 18656848-18656863, 18660288-18660303, 18661104-18661119, 19746704-19746719, 22233904-22233919, 23098368-23098383, 23382992-23383007, 24102464-24102479, 24104240-24104255, 24106656-24106671, 24107456-24107471, 28959968-28959983, 41825776-41825791,

```
41828992-41829007, 52654576-52654591, 52655312-52655327,
60522976-60522991, 68643840-68643855, 69973280-69973295,
72714624-72714639, 72715280-72715295, 82148800-82148815,
83810512-83810527, 85310848-85310863, 85313424-85313439,
85314032-85314047, 86321200-86321215, 86323776-86323791,
87186064-87186079, 87856304-87856319, 87856912-87856927,
97191248-97191263, 100093136-100093151, 103861008-103861023,
109706960-109706991, 110347936-110347951, 110350112-110350127,
115664752-115664767, 115835504-115835519
Source (120103200) has 36198288 fewer sectors than destination (156301488)
Zero fill:                      0
Src Byte fill (ED):             0
Dst Byte fill (F3): 36198288
Other fill:                     0
Other no fill:                  0
Zero fill range:
Src fill range:
Dst fill range:   120103200-156301487
Other fill range:
Other not filled range:
0 source read errors, 0 destination read errors

Actual Date:01/23/07 03:10:59PM
File Integrity:Completely Verified, 0 Errors
Acquisition Hash:474e17967f4d9ccc5a643a21f4907f17
Verify Hash:474e17967f4d9ccc5a643a21f4907f17
EnCase Version:5.05f
System Version:Linux
Error Granularity:16
Read Errors:44
Total Size:61,492,838,400 bytes (57.3GB)
Total Sectors:120,103,200
Read errors:
  10,069,088 (16)
  10,069,904 (16)
  12,023,808 (16)
  18,652,592 (16)
  18,656,032 (16)
  18,656,848 (16)
  18,660,288 (16)
  18,661,104 (16)
  19,746,704 (16)
  22,233,904 (16)
  23,098,368 (16)
  23,382,992 (16)
  24,102,464 (16)
  24,104,240 (16)
  24,106,656 (16)
  24,107,456 (16)
  28,959,968 (16)
  41,825,776 (16)
  41,828,992 (16)
  52,654,576 (16)
  52,655,312 (16)
  60,522,976 (16)
  68,643,840 (16)
  69,973,280 (16)
  72,714,624 (16)
  72,715,280 (16)
  82,148,800 (16)
  83,810,512 (16)
  85,310,848 (16)
  85,313,424 (16)
  85,314,032 (16)
  86,321,200 (16)
  86,323,776 (16)
  87,186,064 (16)
  87,856,304 (16)
  87,856,912 (16)
  97,191,248 (16)
```

Test Case DA-09-16 Linen 5.05f	
	100,093,136 (16) 103,861,008 (16) 109,706,960 (32) 110,347,936 (16) 110,350,112 (16) 115,664,752 (16) 115,835,504 (16)

Results:		
	Assertion & Expected Result	**Actual Result**
	AM-01 Source acquired using interface AI.	as expected
	AM-02 Source is type DS.	as expected
	AM-03 Execution environment is XE.	as expected
	AM-05 An image is created on file system type FS.	as expected
	AM-06 All visible sectors acquired.	as expected
	AM-08 All sectors accurately acquired.	some sectors differ
	AM-09 Error logged.	as expected
	AM-10 Benign fill replaces inaccessible sectors.	as expected
	AO-01 Image file is complete and accurate.	as expected
	AO-05 Multifile image created.	as expected
	AO-22 Tool calculates hashes by block.	option not available
	AO-23 Logged information is correct.	as expected
	AO-24 Source is unchanged by acquisition.	as expected

Analysis:	Expected results not achieved

5.2.22   DA-09-64

Test Case DA-09-64 Linen 5.05f	
Case Summary:	DA-09 Acquire a digital source that has at least one faulty data sector.
Assertions:	AM-01 The tool uses access interface SRC-AI to access the digital source. AM-02 The tool acquires digital source DS. AM-03 The tool executes in execution environment XE. AM-05 If image file creation is specified, the tool creates an image file on file system type FS. AM-06 All visible sectors are acquired from the digital source. AM-08 All sectors acquired from the digital source are acquired accurately. AM-09 If unresolved errors occur while reading from the selected digital source, the tool notifies the user of the error type and location within the digital source. AM-10 If unresolved errors occur while reading from the selected digital source, the tool uses a benign fill in the destination object in place of the inaccessible data. AO-01 If the tool creates an image file, the data represented by the image file is the same as the data acquired by the tool. AO-05 If the tool creates a multi-file image of a requested size then all the individual files shall be no larger than the requested size. AO-22 If requested, the tool calculates block hashes for a specified block size during an acquisition for each block acquired from the digital source. AO-23 If the tool logs any log significant information, the information is accurately recorded in the log file. AO-24 If the tool executes in a forensically safe execution environment, the digital source is unchanged by the acquisition process.
Tester Name:	brl
Test Host:	Paladin
Test Date:	Thu Jan 25 17:15:18 2007
Drives:	src(ED-BAD-CPR1) dst (F0) other (EF)
Source Setup:	No before hash for ED-BAD-CPR1 120103200 total sectors (61492838400 bytes) Drive with known bad sectors Vendor: Maxtor Model: DiamondMax Plus 9 Known Bad Sector List for ED-CPR-BAD-1 Manufacturer: Maxtor Model: 6Y060L0 DiamondMax Plus 9 Serial Number: Y27KR6CE Capacity: 60GB Interface: PATA 10069095, 10069911, 12023808, 18652594, 18656041, 18656857, 18660303, 18661119, 19746716-19746717, 22233904, 23098370, 23383001, 24102466-24102467, 24104250, 24106656, 24107458, 28959971-28959972, 41825791, 41828995, 52654580, 52655318, 60522984, 68643842-68643843, 69973290, 72714626, 72715293, 82148809, 82148810, 83810525, 85310861, 85313430, 85314038-85314039, 86321211, 86323780, 87186066, 87856313, 87856922, 97191260-97191261, 100093150-100093151, 103861021, 109706975-109706976, 110347947, 110350122-110350123, 115664758, 115835518
Log Highlights:	Destination setup 156301488 sectors wiped with F0 Comparision of original to clone Drive Sectors compared: 120103200 Sectors match: 120100384 Sectors differ: 2816 Bytes differ: 1438976 Diffs range 10069056-10069119, 10069888-10069951, 12023808-12023871, 18652544-18652607, 18656000-18656063, 18656832-18656895, 18660288-18660351, 18661056-18661119, 19746688-19746751, 22233856-22233919, 23098368-23098431, 23382976-23383039, 24102464-24102527, 24104192-24104255, 24106624-24106687, 24107456-24107519, 28959936-28959999, 41825728-41825791,

```
41828992-41829055, 52654528-52654591, 52655296-52655359,
60522944-60523007, 68643840-68643903, 69973248-69973311,
72714624-72714687, 72715264-72715327, 82148800-82148863,
83810496-83810559, 85310848-85310911, 85313408-85313471,
85313984-85314047, 86321152-86321215, 86323776-86323839,
87186048-87186111, 87856256-87856319, 87856896-87856959,
97191232-97191295, 100093120-100093183, 103860992-103861055,
109706944-109707007, 110347904-110347967, 110350080-110350143,
115664704-115664767, 115835456-115835519
Source (120103200) has 36198288 fewer sectors than destination (156301488)
Zero fill:                    0
Src Byte fill (ED):           0
Dst Byte fill (F0): 36198288
Other fill:                   0
Other no fill:                0
Zero fill range:
Src fill range:
Dst fill range:   120103200-156301487
Other fill range:
Other not filled range:
0 source read errors, 0 destination read errors

Actual Date:02/06/07 10:57:08AM
File Integrity:Completely Verified, 0 Errors
Acquisition Hash:f7537808758654f5d3bd66d0bc0ee827
Verify Hash:f7537808758654f5d3bd66d0bc0ee827
EnCase Version:5.05f
System Version:Linux
Error Granularity:64
Read Errors:44
Total Size:61,492,838,400 bytes (57.3GB)
Total Sectors:120,103,200
Read errors:
  10,069,056 (64)
  10,069,888 (64)
  12,023,808 (64)
  18,652,544 (64)
  18,656,000 (64)
  18,656,832 (64)
  18,660,288 (64)
  18,661,056 (64)
  19,746,688 (64)
  22,233,856 (64)
  23,098,368 (64)
  23,382,976 (64)
  24,102,464 (64)
  24,104,192 (64)
  24,106,624 (64)
  24,107,456 (64)
  28,959,936 (64)
  41,825,728 (64)
  41,828,992 (64)
  52,654,528 (64)
  52,655,296 (64)
  60,522,944 (64)
  68,643,840 (64)
  69,973,248 (64)
  72,714,624 (64)
  72,715,264 (64)
  82,148,800 (64)
  83,810,496 (64)
  85,310,848 (64)
  85,313,408 (64)
  85,313,984 (64)
  86,321,152 (64)
  86,323,776 (64)
  87,186,048 (64)
  87,856,256 (64)
  87,856,896 (64)
  97,191,232 (64)
```

Test Case DA-09-64 Linen 5.05f	
	100,093,120 (64)
	103,860,992 (64)
	109,706,944 (64)
	110,347,904 (64)
	110,350,080 (64)
	115,664,704 (64)
	115,835,456 (64)

Results:		
	Assertion & Expected Result	**Actual Result**
	AM-01 Source acquired using interface AI.	as expected
	AM-02 Source is type DS.	as expected
	AM-03 Execution environment is XE.	as expected
	AM-05 An image is created on file system type FS.	as expected
	AM-06 All visible sectors acquired.	as expected
	AM-08 All sectors accurately acquired.	some sectors differ
	AM-09 Error logged.	as expected
	AM-10 Benign fill replaces inaccessible sectors.	as expected
	AO-01 Image file is complete and accurate.	as expected
	AO-05 Multifile image created.	as expected
	AO-22 Tool calculates hashes by block.	option not available
	AO-23 Logged information is correct.	as expected
	AO-24 Source is unchanged by acquisition.	as expected

Analysis:	Expected results not achieved

5.2.23 DA-10-UNCOMPRESSED

Test Case DA-10-UNCOMPRESSED Linen 5.05f	
Case Summary:	DA-10 Acquire a digital source to an image file in an alternate format.
Assertions:	AM-01 The tool uses access interface SRC-AI to access the digital source. AM-02 The tool acquires digital source DS. AM-03 The tool executes in execution environment XE. AM-05 If image file creation is specified, the tool creates an image file on file system type FS. AM-06 All visible sectors are acquired from the digital source. AM-08 All sectors acquired from the digital source are acquired accurately. AO-01 If the tool creates an image file, the data represented by the image file is the same as the data acquired by the tool. AO-02 If an image file format is specified, the tool creates an image file in the specified format. AO-05 If the tool creates a multi-file image of a requested size then all the individual files shall be no larger than the requested size. AO-22 If requested, the tool calculates block hashes for a specified block size during an acquisition for each block acquired from the digital source. AO-23 If the tool logs any log significant information, the information is accurately recorded in the log file. AO-24 If the tool executes in a forensically safe execution environment, the digital source is unchanged by the acquisition process.
Tester Name:	brl
Test Host:	Aramis
Test Date:	Thu Feb 8 06:09:12 2007
Drives:	src(41) dst (none) other (52-IDE)
Source Setup:	src hash (SHA1): < 15CAA1A307271160D8372668BF8A03FC45A51CC9 > src hash (MD5): < 0A6A8EF78BDC14E2026710D8CCB5607C > 78125000 total sectors (40000000000 bytes) 65534/015/63 (max cyl/hd values) 65535/016/63 (number of cyl/hd) IDE disk: Model (WDC WD400BB-75JHC0) serial # (WD-WMAMC4658355) N Start LBA Length Start C/H/S End C/H/S boot Partition type 1 P 000000063 078107967 0000/001/01 1023/254/63 Boot 07 NTFS 2 P 000000000 000000000 0000/000/00 0000/000/00 00 empty entry 3 P 000000000 000000000 0000/000/00 0000/000/00 00 empty entry 4 P 000000000 000000000 0000/000/00 0000/000/00 00 empty entry 1 078107967 sectors 39991279104 bytes
Log Highlights:	Actual Date:02/08/07 06:14:52AM File Integrity:Completely Verified, 0 Errors Acquisition Hash:0a6a8ef78bdc14e2026710d8ccb5607c Verify Hash:0a6a8ef78bdc14e2026710d8ccb5607c EnCase Version:5.05f System Version:Linux Error Granularity:64 Total Size:40,000,000,000 bytes (37.3GB) Total Sectors:78,125,000 Rehash of Source MD5: 0A6A8EF78BDC14E2026710D8CCB5607C

<table>
<tr><td rowspan="13">Results:</td><td colspan="2"></td></tr>
<tr><td>Assertion & Expected Result</td><td>Actual Result</td></tr>
<tr><td>AM-01 Source acquired using interface AI.</td><td>as expected</td></tr>
<tr><td>AM-02 Source is type DS.</td><td>as expected</td></tr>
<tr><td>AM-03 Execution environment is XE.</td><td>as expected</td></tr>
<tr><td>AM-05 An image is created on file system type FS.</td><td>as expected</td></tr>
<tr><td>AM-06 All visible sectors acquired.</td><td>as expected</td></tr>
<tr><td>AM-08 All sectors accurately acquired.</td><td>as expected</td></tr>
<tr><td>AO-01 Image file is complete and accurate.</td><td>as expected</td></tr>
<tr><td>AO-02 Image file in specified format.</td><td>as expected</td></tr>
<tr><td>AO-05 Multifile image created.</td><td>as expected</td></tr>
<tr><td>AO-22 Tool calculates hashes by block.</td><td>option not available</td></tr>
<tr><td>AO-23 Logged information is correct.</td><td>as expected</td></tr>
<tr><td>AO-24 Source is unchanged by acquisition.</td><td>as expected</td></tr>
</table>

Test Case DA-10-UNCOMPRESSED Linen 5.05f	
Analysis:	Expected results achieved

5.2.24 DA-13

Test Case DA-13 Linen 5.05f	
Case Summary:	DA-13 Create an image file where there is insufficient space on a single volume, and use destination device switching to continue on another volume.
Assertions:	AM-01 The tool uses access interface SRC-AI to access the digital source. AM-02 The tool acquires digital source DS. AM-03 The tool executes in execution environment XE. AM-05 If image file creation is specified, the tool creates an image file on file system type FS. AM-06 All visible sectors are acquired from the digital source. AM-08 All sectors acquired from the digital source are acquired accurately. AO-01 If the tool creates an image file, the data represented by the image file is the same as the data acquired by the tool. AO-04 If the tool is creating an image file and there is insufficient space on the image destination device to contain the image file, the tool shall notify the user. AO-05 If the tool creates a multi-file image of a requested size then all the individual files shall be no larger than the requested size. AO-10 If there is insufficient space to contain all files of a multi-file image and if destination device switching is supported, the image is continued on another device. AO-22 If requested, the tool calculates block hashes for a specified block size during an acquisition for each block acquired from the digital source. AO-23 If the tool logs any log significant information, the information is accurately recorded in the log file. AO-24 If the tool executes in a forensically safe execution environment, the digital source is unchanged by the acquisition process.
Tester Name:	brl
Test Host:	Max
Test Date:	Mon Feb 12 11:35:37 2007
Drives:	src(07) dst (61-FU2) other (82-FU2)
Source Setup:	src hash (SHA1): < 655E9BDDB36A3F9C5C4CC8BF32B8C5B41AF9F52E > src hash (MD5): < 2EAF712DAD80F66E30DEA00365B4579B > 156301488 total sectors (80026361856 bytes) Model (WDC WD800JD-32HK) serial # (WD-WMAJ91510044) N Start LBA Length Start C/H/S End C/H/S boot Partition type 1 P 000000063 156280257 0000/001/01 1023/254/63 Boot 07 NTFS 2 P 000000000 000000000 0000/000/00 0000/000/00 00 empty entry 3 P 000000000 000000000 0000/000/00 0000/000/00 00 empty entry 4 P 000000000 000000000 0000/000/00 0000/000/00 00 empty entry 1 156280257 sectors 80015491584 bytes
Log Highlights:	Actual Date:02/09/07 10:58:37AM File Integrity:Completely Verified, 0 Errors Acquisition Hash:2eaf712dad80f66e30dea00365b4579b Verify Hash:2eaf712dad80f66e30dea00365b4579b EnCase Version:5.05f System Version:Linux Error Granularity:64 Total Size:80,026,361,856 bytes (74.5GB) Total Sectors:156,301,488 Rehash of Source MD5: 2EAF712DAD80F66E30DEA00365B4579B
Results:	

Assertion & Expected Result	Actual Result
AM-01 Source acquired using interface AI.	as expected
AM-02 Source is type DS.	as expected
AM-03 Execution environment is XE.	as expected
AM-05 An image is created on file system type FS.	as expected
AM-06 All visible sectors acquired.	as expected
AM-08 All sectors accurately acquired.	as expected
AO-01 Image file is complete and accurate.	as expected
AO-04 User notified if space exhausted.	as expected
AO-05 Multifile image created.	as expected
AO-10 Image file continued on new device.	as expected

Test Case DA-13 Linen 5.05f		
	AO-22 Tool calculates hashes by block.	option not available
	AO-23 Logged information is correct.	as expected
	AO-24 Source is unchanged by acquisition.	as expected
Analysis:	Expected results achieved	

About the National Institute of Justice

NIJ is the research, development, and evaluation agency of the U.S. Department of Justice. NIJ's mission is to advance scientific research, development, and evaluation to enhance the administration of justice and public safety. NIJ's principal authorities are derived from the Omnibus Crime Control and Safe Streets Act of 1968, as amended (see 42 U.S.C. §§ 3721–3723).

The NIJ Director is appointed by the President and confirmed by the Senate. The Director establishes the Institute's objectives, guided by the priorities of the Office of Justice Programs, the U.S. Department of Justice, and the needs of the field. The Institute actively solicits the views of criminal justice and other professionals and researchers to inform its search for the knowledge and tools to guide policy and practice.

Strategic Goals

NIJ has seven strategic goals grouped into three categories:

Creating relevant knowledge and tools

1. Partner with State and local practitioners and policymakers to identify social science research and technology needs.
2. Create scientific, relevant, and reliable knowledge—with a particular emphasis on terrorism, violent crime, drugs and crime, cost-effectiveness, and community-based efforts—to enhance the administration of justice and public safety.
3. Develop affordable and effective tools and technologies to enhance the administration of justice and public safety.

Dissemination

4. Disseminate relevant knowledge and information to practitioners and policymakers in an understandable, timely, and concise manner.
5. Act as an honest broker to identify the information, tools, and technologies that respond to the needs of stakeholders.

Agency management

6. Practice fairness and openness in the research and development process.
7. Ensure professionalism, excellence, accountability, cost-effectiveness, and integrity in the management and conduct of NIJ activities and programs.

Program Areas

In addressing these strategic challenges, the Institute is involved in the following program areas: crime control and prevention, including policing; drugs and crime; justice systems and offender behavior, including corrections; violence and victimization; communications and information technologies; critical incident response; investigative and forensic sciences, including DNA; less-than-lethal technologies; officer protection; education and training technologies; testing and standards; technology assistance to law enforcement and corrections agencies; field testing of promising programs; and international crime control.

In addition to sponsoring research and development and technology assistance, NIJ evaluates programs, policies, and technologies. NIJ communicates its research and evaluation findings through conferences and print and electronic media.

To find out more about the National Institute of Justice, please visit:

http://www.ojp.usdoj.gov/nij

or contact:

National Criminal Justice
 Reference Service
P.O. Box 6000
Rockville, MD 20849–6000
800–851–3420
e-mail: *askncjrs@ncjrs.org*